Advantage Computer Concepts

A Brief Introduction to Hardware, Software and Communications

Sarah E. Hutchinson

Glen J. Coulthard

Stacey C. Sawyer

THE ADVANTAGE SERIES FOR COMPUTER EDUCATION

Irwin
McGraw-Hill

Boston, Massachusetts · Burr Ridge, Illinois · Dubuque, Iowa
Madison, Wisconsin · New York, New York · San Francisco, California · St. Louis, Missouri

Irwin/McGraw-Hill

A Division of The McGraw-Hill Companies

COMPUTER CONCEPTS: A Brief Introduction to Hardware, Software and Communications

Microsoft, © PowerPoint and Windows are registered trademarks of the Microsoft Corporation.

7 8 9 0 WEB/WEB 9 0 4 3 2

ISBN 0-07-289508-X

Vice president and editorial director: *Michael W. Junior*
Senior sponsoring editor: *Garrett Glanz*
Developmental editor: *Kristin Moore*
Marketing manager: *James Rogers*
Senior project manager: *Denise Santor-Mitzit*
Senior production supervisor: *Melonie Salvati*
Designer: *Laurie J. Entringer*
Compositor: *GTS Graphics*
Typeface: *11/13 Bodoni Book*
Printer: *Webcrafters, Inc.*

http://www.mhhe.com

WELCOME TO THE IRWIN ADVANTAGE SERIES

The Irwin Advantage Series has evolved over the years to become one of the most respected resources for software training in the world, and now you've chosen to complement your software instruction with a brief overview of computer concepts. This guide is intended to provide a basic introduction to computers. It will stimulate and enhance understanding as students prepare to use software applications. Our instructional methodologies are proven to optimize the student's ability to learn, yet we continually seek ways to improve on our products and approach. To this end, all our learning guides are classroom tested and critically reviewed by dozens of learners, teachers, and software training experts. We're glad you have chosen the Irwin Advantage Series!

KEY FEATURES

The following features are incorporated into this guide to ensure that your learning experience is as productive and enjoyable as possible:

LEARNING OBJECTIVES

The guide begins by outlining the concepts and skills to be learned. Students can easily identify what will be expected of them before delving into the material.

QUICK CHECKS

After every major topic, concepts are reinforced with a short answer question. These simple questions encourage independent thinking and ensure comprehension of the current topic before students proceed to the next section.

EXERCISES

This guide ends with *key terms, short answer questions, true/false questions, multiple choice questions, and knowledge in action exercises.* These comprehensive and meaningful exercises are integrated with the book's objectives. They serve to provide students with opportunities to practice the session material. For maximum benefit, students should complete all the exercises.

TEXT SUPPLEMENTS

INSTRUCTOR'S RESOURCE KIT

For instructors and software trainers, each learning guide is accompanied by an *Instructor's Resource Kit* (IRK). This kit provides suggested answers to the short-answer questions, hands-on exercises, and case problems appearing at the end of each session. Futhermore, the IRK includes a comprehensive test bank of additional short-answer, multiple-choice, and fill-in-the-blank questions.

ACKNOWLEDGMENTS

The Advantage Series of learning guides is the direct result of the teamwork and spirit of many people. We sincerely thank the reviewers, instructors, and students who have shared their comments and suggestions with us over past years. With the valuable feedback, our guides have evolved into the product you see before you. We also appreciate the efforts of the instructors and students at Okanagan University College who classroom tested our guides to ensure accuracy, relevancy, and completeness.

We also give many thanks to Garrett Glanz, Kristin Moore and Mike Junior from Irwin/McGraw-Hill for their skillful management of this text. In fact, special recognition goes to all the individuals mentioned in the credits at the beginning of this guide. And finally, to the many others who weren't directly involved in this project but who have stood by us the whole way, we appreciate your encouragement and support.

WRITE TO US

We welcome your response to this guide, for we are trying to make it as useful a learning tool as possible. Write to us in care of Garrett Glanz, Irwin/McGraw-Hill, 1333 Burr Ridge Parkway, Burr Ridge, IL 60521. Thank you.

Sarah E. Hutchinson
sclifford@mindspring.com

Glen J. Coulthard
glen@coulthard.com

Stacey C. Sawyer
staceys@mindspring.com

Contents

Computers:
A Brief Overview

OUTLINE

LEARNING OBJECTIVES

After completing this guide, you will be able to:

- Define *computer,* and explain what *analog* and *digital* mean.
- Name the six elements in a computer-and-communications system.
- Describe the main types of computers and their uses.
- Identify and evaluate a computer in terms of its input, processing, storage, output, and communications and hardware components.
- Explain the importance of *system software* and *applications software,* and name some common types of each.
- Describe the significance of the Internet and the World Wide Web (WWW).

WHAT IS A COMPUTER?

In the first part of this century, computers were people—persons who compute—and machines that computed were calculators. However, after about 1940, human computers began to be replaced by machines called "electronic computers." Today the term **computer** describes a device made up of a combination of electronic and electromechanical (part electronic; part mechanical) components. By itself, a computer has no intelligence and is referred to as **hardware,** which simply means the physical equipment. The hardware can't be used until it is connected to other elements, all of which constitute the six parts of a **computer-based information system.** *(See Figure 1.)*

Software is the term used to describe the instructions or programs that tell the hardware how to perform a task. Without software, the hardware is useless.

Computer-based information systems are used in most businesses today to perform repetitive tasks and to transform data into information that can be used by people to make decisions, sell products, and perform a variety of other activities. Data can be considered the raw materials—whether in paper, electronic, or other form—that is processed by the computer. In other words, **data** consists of the raw facts and figures that are processed into information. **Information** is summarized data or otherwise manipulated (processed) data. For example, the raw data of

FIGURE 1

A computer-based information system typically combines six elements.

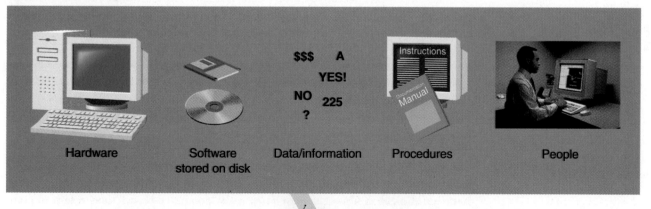

Hardware   Software stored on disk   Data/information   Procedures   People

Communications (connectivity)

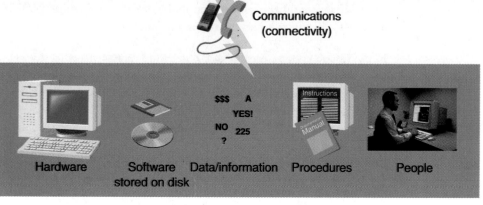

Hardware   Software stored on disk   Data/information   Procedures   People

employees' hours worked and wage rates is processed by a computer into the information of paychecks and payroll reports.

People, however, constitute the most important component of the computer system. People operate the computer hardware, and they create, customize, and use the computer software. They enter the data and use the information the system generates. They also follow certain procedures when using the hardware and software. **Procedures** are descriptions of how things are done, or steps for accomplishing a task or result. Procedures for computer systems appear in printed and online **documentation manuals,** also know as reference manuals and user guides, which contain instructions, rules, and guidelines to follow when using hardware and software.

When one computer is set up to share data and information electronically with another computer system, **communications**—also called **connectivity**—becomes a sixth system element. In other words, the manner in which the various individual systems are connected—for example, by a cable or wire, phone lines, microwave transmission, or satellite—is an element of the total computer system.

One of the main characteristics of a computer is its digital nature. No doubt you're used to hearing the word "digital" often, but what does it really mean? We explore the answer to this question in the next section.

THE DIGITAL BASIS OF COMPUTERS

Computers may seem like incredibly complicated devices, but their underlying principle is simple. When you look inside a microcomputer, what you see is mainly electronic circuitry. And what is the most basic statement that can be made about electricity? Simply this—it can be either *turned on* or *turned off.*

In a two-state on/off, open/closed, positive/negative arrangement, one state can represent a 1 digit, the other a 0 digit. People are most comfortable with the decimal number system, which has ten digits (0, 1, 2, 3, 4, 5, 6, 7, 8, 9). Because computers are based on on/off or other two-state conditions, they use the **binary number system,** which consists of only two digits—0 and 1.

The word *digit* simply means "numeral." The word *digital* is derived from "digit," which refers to our fingers that people still sometimes use to count with. Today, however, **digital** is almost synonymous with "computer-based" and refers to communications signals or information represented in a discrete (individually distinct) form—usually in a binary or two-state way.

In the binary system, each 0 and 1 is called a **bit**—short for **binary digit.** In turn, bits can be grouped in various combinations to represent characters of data—numbers, letters, punctuation marks, and so on. For example, the letter *H* could correspond to the electronic signal 01001000 (that is, off-on-off-off-on-off-off-off). In computing, a group of 8 bits is called a **byte,** and each character is represented by 1 byte.

Digital data, then, consists of data in discrete, discontinuous form—usually 0s and 1s. This is the method of data representation by which computers process and store data and communicate with one another.

THE ANALOG BASIS OF LIFE

Most phenomena of the world are not digital: they are **analog,** having continuously variable values. Sound, light, temperature, and pressure values, for instance, can fall anywhere on a continuum or range. The highs, lows, and in-between states have historically been represented with analog devices, such as pressure sensors and thermometers, rather than in digital form. Thus, analog data is transmitted in a continuous form—a wave-like pattern—that closely resembles the information it represents. The electrical signals on a telephone line are analog-data representations of the original voices. Telephone, radio, broadcast television, and cable TV have traditionally transmitted analog data.

The differences between analog and digital data transmission are apparent when you look at a drawing of a wavy analog signal, such as a voice message on a standard telephone line, and an on/off digital signal. *(See Figure 2.)* To transmit your computer's digital signals over telephone lines, you usually need to use a *modem* to translate them into analog signals. (The word *modem* comes from *mo*dulate/*dem*odulate. To modulate a signal means to convert it from digital to analog form, whereas to demodulate means to convert the signal from analog to digital form.) The **modem** provides a means for computers to send data and to communicate with one another while the old-fashioned copper-wire telephone network—an analog system built to transmit the human voice—still exists.

Communications technology is covered in more detail later on. For now, let's focus on the different types of computers and the basics of computer hardware.

QUICK CHECK	Why must you use a modem to send data over traditional telephone lines?

FIGURE 2

(*Top*) On an analog watch, the hands move continuously around the watch face; on a digital watch, the display changes once each minute. (*Bottom*) Note the wavy line for an analog signal and the on/off line for a digital signal. The modem shown here is outside the computer. Today many modems are inside the computer and thus not visible.

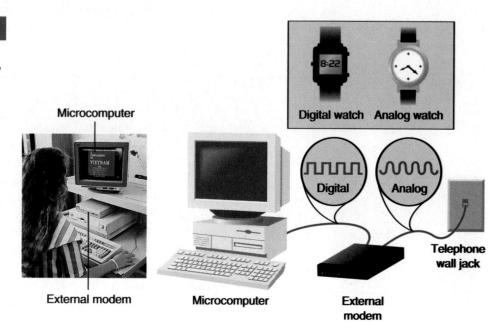

Microcomputer

External modem   Microcomputer   External modem

Digital watch   Analog watch

Digital   Analog

Telephone wall jack

TYPES OF COMPUTERS

Computers have come a long way since the first operational computer in 1940. In 1969 the onboard guidance computer used by the Apollo 11 astronauts, who made the first moon landing, weighed 70 pounds (31 kilograms) and could hold the equivalent of a mere 2000 characters (bytes) of data in its main memory. The Mission Control computer on the ground had only 1 million characters of memory. It cost $4 million and took up most of a room.

Fast forward to the present: Today the shrinkage of computer components means that you can easily buy, for about two thousand dollars, a personal computer that sits on a desktop and has hundreds of times the processing power and about 32 to 64 times the memory of the 1969 Mission Control computer. You have more productivity at your fingertips than the American space program had a generation ago. And computer processing power has traditionally doubled at a rate of every 18 months—a fact often referred to as *Moore's Law.* In other words, the Pentium computer that you just took out of the box will be only half as powerful as computers introduced next year.

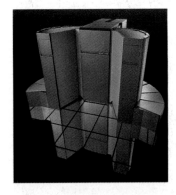

Although you may be familiar only with microcomputers, computers come in a variety of sizes and with a variety of processing capabilities. **Supercomputers** (*top left*) are the fastest and highest-capacity computers. Their cost ranges from several hundreds of thousands to millions of dollars. Among their uses are worldwide weather forecasting, oil exploration, aircraft design, and evaluation of aging nuclear weapons systems. Unlike microcomputers, which generally have only one main processing unit, supercomputers have hundreds to thousands of processors.

Mainframe computers (*middle left*) are less powerful than supercomputers, but they are still fast, mid- to large-size, large-capacity, multi-processor machines. Their size varies depending on how many concurrent users they are serving—from a few hundred to thousands of people. Mainframes are used by many banks, airlines, insurance companies, mail-order houses, universities, and the Internal Revenue Service.

Workstations are expensive, powerful desktop computers used mainly by engineers, scientists, and special-effects creators for sophisticated purposes. Workstations are used for such tasks as modeling airplane fuselages, designing prescription drugs, and creating digital video and animation sequences. The capabilities of low-end workstations overlap those of high-end microcomputers. **Microcomputers** (*bottom left*), also called **personal computers (PCs),** are small computers that can fit on the floor next to a desk, on a desktop, or can be carried around. Whether desktop, tower (floor-standing), notebook, or palmtop, personal computers are now found in most businesses. *(See Figure 3.)* A **local area network (LAN)** connects, using a special cable, a group of desktop PCs and other devices in an office or building for the purpose of sharing data and other physical resources. In most LANs, one PC is assigned the role of **server,** meaning that it stores data and software for use by the other PCs and/or performs services for them, such as database management and printing.

Some companies use a combination of computers, and, indeed, the predominant information system is now a hybrid model, whereby a variety of systems are tied together under a common umbrella. For instance, an insurance company with branch offices around the country might use a mainframe computer to manage companywide customer data. To access information from the mainframe, a local claims adjuster might use a microcomputer on his or her desktop. That same microcomputer can also be used to perform specialized tasks such as generating invoices or drafting letters to customers. Because microcomputers are generally versatile, increasingly powerful, and more affordable than the other types of computers, they are practical tools for organizations wishing to improve their productivity.

FIGURE 3   Microcomputers come in different sizes.

Types of Microcomputers

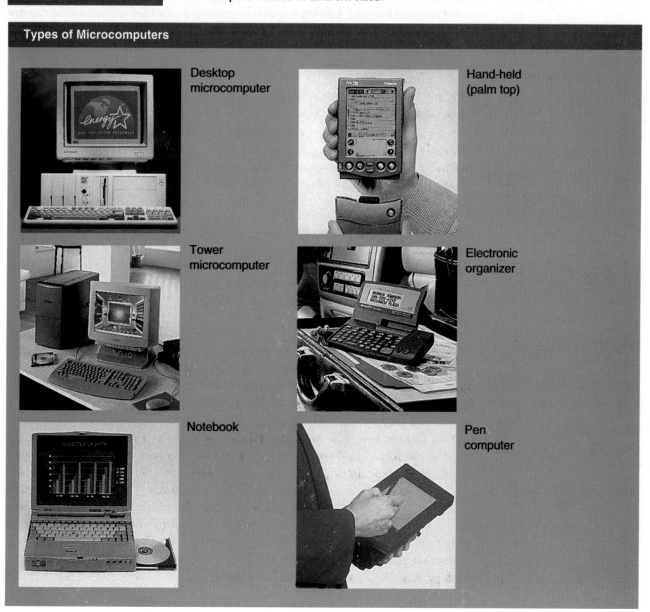

Desktop microcomputer

Hand-held (palm top)

Tower microcomputer

Electronic organizer

Notebook

Pen computer

QUICK CHECK   **What type of computer would you recommend that your friends purchase for their new home-based video production business? What other type(s) of computers could you envision them using?**

COMPUTER HARDWARE

As you already know, the word *hardware* refers to the machinery and equipment of a computer system. Hardware—what most people think of when they visualize a computer system—consists of, among other things, the keyboard, screen, printer, and the computer or processing device itself. In general, computer hardware is categorized according to which of the five computer operations it performs. *(See Figure 4.)* In addition to being categorized according to operation, all external devices that are connected to the computer cabinet but are not inside the main cabinet are referred to as **peripheral devices.** Thus keyboards, mice, monitors, and printers are all peripheral devices.

FIGURE 4

The five categories of computer hardware

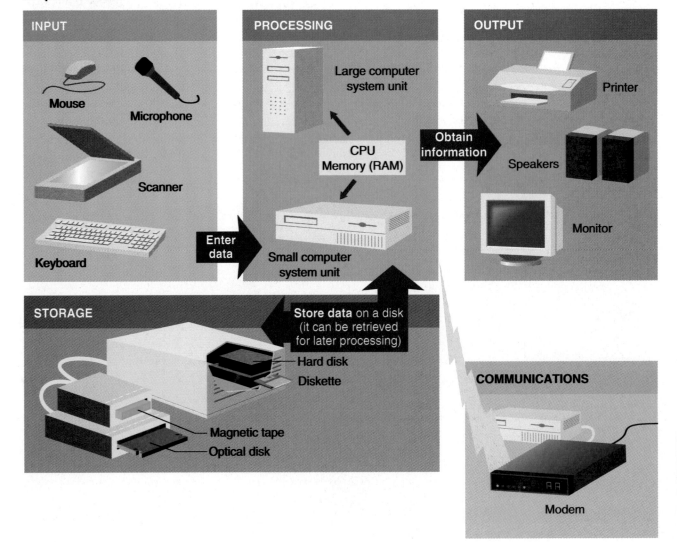

INPUT HARDWARE

The function of **input hardware** is to accept data and convert it into a form suitable for computer processing. In other words, input hardware allows people to put data into the computer in a form that the computer can use. Three commonly used input devices are the keyboard, mouse, and scanner.

Keyboard

A **keyboard** includes the standard typewriter-like keys plus a number of special keys *(see Figure 5 on the next page)*. The standard keys are used mostly to enter words and numbers. The **Enter key** (bent left arrow), sometimes called the Return key, is used to enter commands into the computer, in addition to beginning a new paragraph in most applications software. Other specialized keys include cursor movement keys and function keys labeled F1, F2, and so on. **Function keys** are used to enter software-specific commands.

Mouse

A **mouse** is a pointing device that is rolled about on a desktop to direct a pointer on the computer's display screen. The pointer is a symbol, usually an arrow, that is used to select items from lists (menus) on the screen or to position the cursor. The **cursor,** also called the insertion point, is the symbol on the screen that shows where data may be entered next, such as typing text in a document.

On the bottom side of the mouse is a ball that translates the mouse movement into digital signals. On the top side are one or more buttons. Your software determines the use of the additional buttons: The first one is used for common functions, such as *clicking* and *dragging. (See Figure 6 on page 11.)* Other common pointing devices include the **trackball,** the **joystick,** the **touchpad,** and the **digitizing tablet.**

FIGURE 5   Common keyboard layout

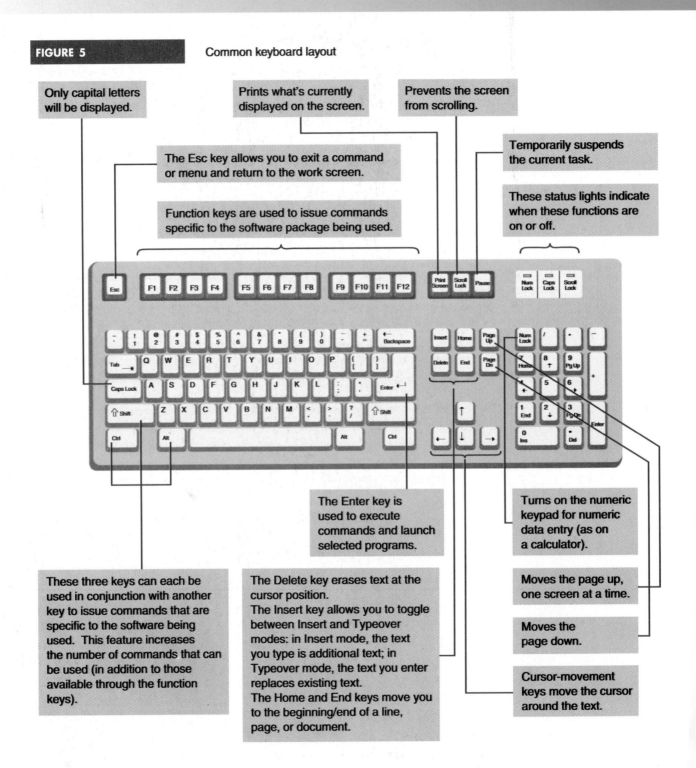

Only capital letters will be displayed.

Prints what's currently displayed on the screen.

Prevents the screen from scrolling.

The Esc key allows you to exit a command or menu and return to the work screen.

Temporarily suspends the current task.

Function keys are used to issue commands specific to the software package being used.

These status lights indicate when these functions are on or off.

The Enter key is used to execute commands and launch selected programs.

Turns on the numeric keypad for numeric data entry (as on a calculator).

These three keys can each be used in conjunction with another key to issue commands that are specific to the software being used. This feature increases the number of commands that can be used (in addition to those available through the function keys).

The Delete key erases text at the cursor position.
The Insert key allows you to toggle between Insert and Typeover modes: in Insert mode, the text you type is additional text; in Typeover mode, the text you enter replaces existing text.
The Home and End keys move you to the beginning/end of a line, page, or document.

Moves the page up, one screen at a time.

Moves the page down.

Cursor-movement keys move the cursor around the text.

FIGURE 6

LEARNING MOUSE LANGUAGE

Term	Definition
	The directions you are most likely to encounter for using a mouse or a trackball are the following:
Point	Move the pointer to the desired spot on the screen, such as over a particular word or object.
Click	Tap—that is, press and quickly release—the left mouse button.
Double-click	Tap—press and release—the left mouse button twice, as quickly as possible.
Drag	Press and hold the left mouse button while moving the pointer to another location.
Drop	Release the mouse button after dragging.
Right-click	Press the right mouse button.

Scanner

Scanners—often used in desktop publishing—translate images of text, drawings, and photos into digital form. The images can then be processed by a computer, displayed on a monitor, inserted in documents, stored on a storage device, or transmitted to another computer. Other scanning devices include *bar-code readers, optical character recognition (OCR) devices,* and *fax machines.*

Although beyond the scope of this guide, there are several other forms of input hardware, including *voice recognition systems, audio-input devices, video capture cards,* and *digital cameras.*

PROCESSING HARDWARE

After data has been input, how is it processed into information? This is the job of the circuitry known as the **processor.** In large computers such as mainframes, this device, along with main memory and some other basic circuitry, is also called the **central processing unit (CPU);** in microcomputers, it is often called the **microprocessor.** The processor works hand in hand with other circuits known as *main memory* and *registers* to carry out processing. Together these circuits form a closed world, which is opened only by connection to input/output devices.

The Processor

The main processor follows the instructions of the software to manipulate data into information. The processor consists of two parts: (1) the control unit and (2) the arithmetic/logic unit. The two components are connected by a kind of electronic roadway called a *bus. (See Figure 7.)* (A bus also connects these components with other parts of the microcomputer, as we will discuss.)

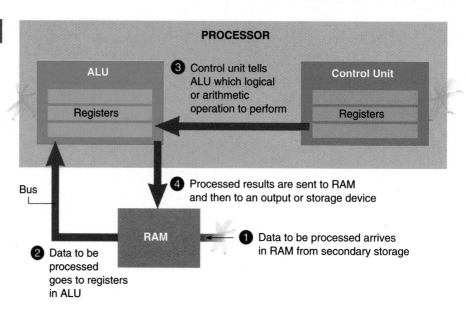

FIGURE 7

The control unit and the arithmetic/logic unit. The two components are connected by a kind of electronic roadway called a *bus.* A bus also connects these components to main memory. Temporary data storage holding/computation working areas called *registers* are located in the control unit and the arithmetic/logic unit.

PROCESSOR

ALU

Registers

3 Control unit tells ALU which logical or arithmetic operation to perform

Control Unit

Registers

Bus

4 Processed results are sent to RAM and then to an output or storage device

RAM

1 Data to be processed arrives in RAM from secondary storage

2 Data to be processed goes to registers in ALU

- *Control unit:* The **control unit** tells the rest of the computer system how to carry out a program's instructions. It directs the movement of electronic signals between main memory and the arithmetic/logic unit. It also directs these electronic signals between main memory and the input and output devices.

- *Arithmetic/logic unit:* The **arithmetic/logic unit,** or **ALU,** performs arithmetic operations and logical operations and controls the speed of those operations. As you might guess, *arithmetic* operations are the fundamental math operations: addition, subtractions, multiplication, and division. *Logical* operations are comparisons. That is, the ALU compares two pieces of data to see whether one is equal to (=), greater than (>), or less than (<) the other. The comparisons can also be combined, as in "greater than or equal to" (>=) and "less than or equal to" (<=).

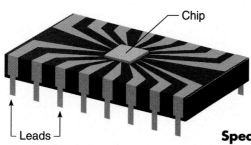

Chip

Leads carry signals to and from the chip

In the most powerful computers, the processor is contained on several relatively large printed circuit boards. In the case of a microcomputer's microprocessor, the processor circuitry is etched on a thumbnail-size or slightly larger **chip** of silicon. The chip is mounted on a carrier with metal leads, or pins, on the bottom that plug into the computer's main circuit board, called the *motherboard,* or the *system board. (See Figure 8.)*

Specialized Processor Chips: Assistants to the CPU

Modern computers may have a number of processors in addition to the main processor. Each of the **coprocessors** is dedicated to a special job. Two common examples are math and graphics coprocessor chips. A *math coprocessor chip* helps programs using lots of mathematical equations to run faster. A *graphics coprocessor chip,* also called a *graphics hardware accelerator,* enhances the performance of programs with lots of graphics and helps create complex screen displays. Specialized chips significantly increase the speed of a computer system by offloading work

FIGURE 8

Motherboard. One main component is the microprocessor.

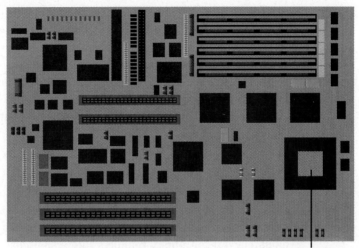

Microprocessor chip

from the main processor. These chips may be plugged directly into the motherboard; however, often they are included on "daughter cards," such as sound cards and graphics cards, used to expand a computer's capabilities.

Main Memory: Working Area for the CPU

Main memory—also known as *memory, primary storage, internal memory,* or *RAM (random access memory)*—is working storage. The term *random access* comes from the fact that data can be stored and retrieved at random—from anywhere in the electronic RAM chips—in approximately equal amounts of time, no matter what the specific data locations are. Main memory is in effect the computer's short-term storage capacity. It determines the total size of the programs and data files it can work on at any given moment. There are two important facts to know about main memory:

- *Its capacity varies in different computers:* The size of main memory is important. It determines how much data can be processed at once and how big and complex a program may be used to process it.

- *Its contents are temporary:* Once the power to the computer is turned off, all the data and programs within main memory simply vanish. Thus, main memory is said to be "volatile," because the contents are lost when the power is turned off. Consequently, if you kick out the connecting power cord to your computer, whatever you are currently working on will immediately disappear. This is why programs and data must also be stored permanently on disks and tapes, called *secondary storage* to distinguish them from main memory's *primary storage.* This impermanence is also the reason why you should *frequently* save your work in progress to a secondary-storage medium every 3–5 minutes, or after major modifications.

Main memory is contained on components called *RAM chips.* Memory chips are typically grouped on *single in-line memory modules,* or *SIMMs,* small circuit boards inserted into slots inside the computer and connected to the processor by a bus. Common RAM technologies are dynamic RAM (DRAM), static RAM (SRAM), and extended data out (EDO) RAM.

Registers

The control unit and the ALU also contain **registers,** or special high-speed circuitry areas that temporarily store data during processing and provide the working areas for computation. It could be said that main memory, which is outside the processor, holds material that will be used "a little bit later." Registers, which are contained in the processor, hold material that is to be processed "immediately." The computer loads the program instructions and data from main memory into the registers just before processing.

Machine Language: The Language of the Processor

All the amazing things that computers do are based on binary numbers made up of 0s and 1s. The binary digits, bits, are stored as charged and uncharged memory cells in the computer's main memory. On magnetic disk and tape, the bits are stored as positively and negatively charged magnetic spots. Display screens and printers convert the binary numbers into visual characters. However, the data that we enter to the computer is not input as random groupings of 0s and 1s: They are encoded, or arranged by means of *binary,* or *digital, coding schemes* to represent letters, numbers, and special characters.

There are many coding schemes. Two common ones are *EBCDIC* and *ASCII-8.* Both use 8 bits to form each byte. *(See Figure 9.)*

- *EBCDIC:* Pronounced "*eb*-see-dick," **EBCDIC,** which stands for **Extended Binary Coded Decimal Interchange Code,** is commonly used in large computers.

- *ASCII-8* or *"extended ASCII":* Pronounced "*as*-key," **ASCII,** which stands for **American Standard for Code for Information Interchange,** is the most widely used binary code with microcomputers.

FIGURE 9					
Character	**ASCII-8**	**EBCDIC**	**Character**	**ASCII-8**	**EBCDIC**
A	0100 0001	1100 0001	N	0100 1110	1101 0101
B	0100 0010	1100 0010	O	0100 1111	1101 0110
C	0100 0011	1100 0011	P	0101 0000	1101 0111
D	0100 0100	1100 0100	Q	0101 0001	1101 1000
E	0100 0101	1100 0101	R	0101 0010	1101 1001
F	0100 0110	1100 0110	S	0101 0011	1110 0010
G	0100 0111	1100 0111	T	0101 0100	1110 0011
H	0100 1000	1100 1000	U	0101 0101	1110 0100
I	0100 1001	1100 1001	V	0101 0110	1110 0101
J	0100 1010	1101 0001	W	0101 0111	1110 0110
K	0100 1011	1101 0010	X	0101 1000	1110 0111
L	0100 1100	1101 0011	Y	0101 1001	1110 1000
M	0100 1101	1101 0100	Z	0101 1010	1110 1001
0	0011 0000	1111 0000	5	0011 0101	1111 0101
1	0011 0001	1111 0001	6	0011 0110	1111 0110
2	0011 0010	1111 0010	7	0011 0111	1111 0111
3	0011 0011	1111 0011	8	0011 1000	1111 1000
4	0011 0100	1111 0100	9	0011 1001	1111 1001
!	0010 0001	0101 1010	;	0011 1011	0101 1110

Two binary coding schemes: ASCII and EBCDIC. There are many more characters than are shown here. These include punctuation marks, Greek letters, math symbols, and foreign language characters.

But if data is represented this way in all microcomputers, why won't word processing software that runs on an Apple Macintosh run (without special arrangements) on an IBM PC? In other words, why are these two microcomputer platforms incompatible? It is because each hardware platform, or processor model family, has a unique machine language.

Machine language is a binary programming language that the computer can run directly. To most people an instruction written in machine language is incomprehensible, consisting only of 0s and 1s. However, it is what the computer itself can understand, and the 0s and 1s represent precise storage locations and operations. The two most popular microcomputer platforms include Intel processors, used in most IBM-type microcomputers, and Motorola processors, used in Macintoshes and other Apple microcomputers.

Many people are initially confused by the difference between the 0 and 1 ASCII code used for data representation and the 0 and 1 used in machine language. What's the difference? ASCII is used for *data* files—that is, files containing only data in the form of ASCII code. Data files cannot be opened and worked on without *execution* programs, the software instructions that tell the computer what to do with the data files. These execution programs are run by the computer in the form of machine language.

But wouldn't it be horrendously difficult for programmers to write complex software programs in seemingly endless series of machine-language groups of 0s and 1s? Indeed it would, so they don't. Instead, programmers write in special programming languages that more closely resemble human language. Then, basically, this code is translated by special programs called *language translators* into the machine language that the computer's particular type of processor can "understand." This translating occurs virtually instantaneously, so that you are not aware of its happening.

Memory and Storage Capacity

How many 0s and 1s will a computer's main memory or a storage device such as a hard disk hold? This is a very important matter. The following terms are used to denote capacity:

- *Bit:* In the binary system, the binary digit (bit)—0 or 1—is the smallest unit of measurement.

- *Byte:* To represent letters, numbers, or special characters (such as ! or *), bits are combined into groups. A group of 8 bits is called a byte, and a byte represents one character, digit, or other value. (For example, in one scheme, 01001000 represents the letter *H.*) The capacity of a computer's memory or of a diskette is expressed in numbers of bytes, or generally in multiples of bytes.

- *Kilobyte:* A **kilobyte (K, KB)** is about 1000 bytes. (Actually, it's precisely 1,024 bytes, but the figure is commonly rounded.) The kilobyte was a common unit of measure for memory or secondary-storage capacity on older computers.

- *Megabyte:* A **megabyte (M, MB)** is about 1 million bytes (1,048,576 bytes). Many measures of microcomputer capacity—such as for main memory and diskettes—are expressed in megabytes. Typical main memory configurations for microcomputers are 16 MB, and 32 MB.

- *Gigabyte:* A **gigabyte (G, GB)** is about 1 billion bytes (1,073,741,824 bytes). This measure is used to measure the capacity of many microcomputer hard disks and the main memory capacity of mainframes. Typical hard disk capacities for microcomputers are 2.1 GB and 4.3 GB.

- *Terabyte:* A **terabyte (T, TB)** represents about 1 trillion bytes (1,009,511,627,776 bytes). This unit of measure is used for some supercomputers' main memory capacity.

16-Bit versus 32-Bit Processing

Processor capacity is also expressed in terms of **word size,** which refers to the number of bits the computer can hold in its registers, process at one time, and send through its internal (local) bus, the electronic pathway between the CPU, memory, and the registers. Often the more bits in a word, the faster the computer. An 8-bit processor will work with data and instructions in 8-bit chunks. Other things being equal, a 32-bit computer processes 4 bytes in the same time it takes a 16-bit machine to process 2 bytes.

Note that expansion bus capacity is also measured by word size. Expansion buses connect the processor, RAM, and registers to the computer's daughter cards and peripheral devices. In other words, you can characterize a processor by saying how many bits it can work with at a time *and* how many bits it can send or receive at a time. Thus you can have a microcomputer with a 32-bit local bus but a 16-bit expansion bus. Most microcomputers offer both 32-bit *PCI* expansion buses and 16-bit *ISA* expansion buses for older legacy products.

Measuring Processing Speeds *Hertz*

Computers with a large word size can process more data at once, thus speeding up processing. There are three main ways in which processing speeds are measured:

- *Microcomputers:* Every computer contains a system clock, an internal timing device that switches on when the power to the computer is turned on. The **system clock** controls how fast all the operations take place. The system clock uses fixed vibrations from a quartz crystal to deliver a steady stream of digital pulses to pace the processor. The faster the clock, the faster the processing, assuming the computer's internal circuits can handle the increased speed.

  Microcomputer processing speeds are most often expressed in **megahertz (MHz),** with 1 MHz equal to 1 million beats, or machine cycles, per second. (A *machine cycle* is the shortest interval in which an elementary operation can take place within the processor.) At this speed, 1 machine cycle is executed in 10 billionths of a second (10 nanoseconds). Microcomputers purchased today commonly run at 133–300 MHz or more. High-end microprocessor speeds may occasionally be measured in MIPS. (*See next paragraph.*)

- *Workstations, midsize computers, and mainframes:* Processing speed can also be measured according to the number of instructions processed per second, which today is in the millions. Thus **MIPS (millions of instructions per second)** is a measure of a computer's processing speed. A high-end microcomputer or a workstation might perform at 100 MIPS or higher, a mainframe 200–1200 or more MIPS.

- *Supercomputers:* Supercomputer processing speed is measured in **flops,** which stands for **floating-point operations per second,** a floating-point operation being a special kind of mathematical calculation. This measure is usually expressed in:

  —*megaflops (mflops),* or millions of floating-point operations per second

  —*gigaflops (gflops),* or billions of floating point operations per second (1 billion flops)

  —*teraflops (tflops),* or trillions of floating point operations per second (1 trillion flops)

Consider a supercomputer such as Option Red at Sandia National Laboratories, Albuquerque, New Mexico, which cranks out 1.8 teraflops. In a galaxy of 1000 planets, each planet with as many people as earth, it would take every person in the galaxy, each doing one calculation—at the same time—to equal what the computer can do in 1 second. Or, if you did one arithmetic calculation every second, nonstop, it would take you more than 31,000 years to do what Option Red does in a second.

OUTPUT HARDWARE

The function of output hardware is to provide the user with the means to view and use information produced by the computer system. One of the most common output devices you will encounter is the printer; another is the monitor.

Types of printers

A **printer** is an output device that prints characters, symbols, and perhaps graphics on paper. (The printed output is generally referred to as *hardcopy.*) Printers are categorized according to whether or not the image produced is formed by physical contact of the printer mechanism with the paper. *Impact printers* have contact: *nonimpact printers* do not. An *impact printer* forms characters or images by striking a mechanism such as a print hammer or head against an inked ribbon, leaving an image on paper. Impact printers are disappearing from the corporate workplace; however, you may still come in contact with a *dot-matrix printer* in school labs and in homes. Nonimpact printers, used almost everywhere now, are faster and quieter than impact printers, because they have fewer moving parts and produce better-quality text and images. A *nonimpact printer* forms characters and images without making direct physical contact between the printing mechanism and the paper. Two types of nonimpact printer often used with microcomputers are *laser printers* and *ink-jet printers.*

Similar to a photocopying machine, a **laser printer** uses the principle of dot-matrix printers of creating images with dots. However, these images are created on a drum, treated with a magnetically charged ink-like toner (powder), and then transferred from drum to paper. *(See Figure 10.)* There are good reasons why laser printers are the most common type of printer. They produce sharp, crisp images of both text and graphics, and they are quiet and fast. They can print 4–32 text-only pages per minute for individual microcomputers. (Pages with graphics print more slowly.) They can print in many fonts (type styles and sizes). The more expensive models can print in different colors.

Like laser and dot-matrix printers, ink-jet printers also form images with little dots. **Ink-jet printers** spray small, electrically charged droplets of ink from four nozzles through holes in a matrix at high speed onto paper. Ink-jet printers can print in color and are quieter but they are much less expensive than a color laser printer. However, they are slower (about 1–4 text-only pages per minute) and print in a somewhat lower resolution (300–720 dpi) than laser printers. High-resolution output requires the use of special coated paper, which costs more than regular paper. And, if you are printing color graphics at 720 dpi on an ink-jet printer, it may take 10 minutes for a single page to finish printing! A variation on ink-jet technology is the *bubble-jet printer,* which uses miniature heating elements to force specially formulated inks through print heads with 128 tiny nozzles. The multiple nozzles print fine images at high speeds. This technology is commonly used in portable printers.

A **plotter** is a specialized output device designed to produce high-quality graphics in a variety of colors. Plotters are especially useful for creating maps and architectural drawings, although they may also produce less complicated charts and graphs. The two principal kinds of plotters are flatbed and drum. *(See Figure 11.)*

Installing a Printer/Plotter

Printers and plotters, like other peripheral devices such as mice, scanners, sound cards, and the like must be *installed.* What does this mean? It means that after physically connecting the printer to the computer, you must load the device's software driver to tell the computer what the device is and that it is now attached. A **driver** is a software program that links a peripheral device to the computer's operating system.

Although many common drivers are provided with today's operating systems, newer or proprietary devices often require programmers who understand the device's language to write specific instructions for the device. The driver contains the machine language necessary to activate the device and perform the necessary operations. Drivers may come on disk with the peripheral device, and driver updates are usually accessible from the manufacturer's home page on the World Wide Web. In the case of fundamental peripherals such as the keyboard, diskette drive, and some hard disks, the drivers are included in the computer's BIOS chip. If you purchase a new peripheral—for example, a scanner—the documentation will tell you what steps to follow to install it. Occasionally a new peripheral's driver will be incompatible with some software already on your computer; in this case, call the company's technical support line for advice.

FIGURE 10

Laser Printer

1 The computer's software sends signals to the laser printer to determine where each dot of printing toner is to be placed on the paper.

2 The instructions from the printer's processor rapidly turn on and off a beam of light from a laser.

3 A spinning mirror deflects the laser beam so that the path of the beam is a horizontal line across the surface of a cylinder called the *drum*. The combination of the laser beam being turned on and off and the movement of the beam's path across the cylinder results in many tiny points of light hitting in a line across the surface of the drum. When the laser has finished flashing points of light across the entire width of the drum, the drum rotates—usually 1/600th of an inch in most laser printers—and the laser beam begins working on the next line of dots.

4 At the same time that the drum begins to rotate, a series of gears and rollers feeds a sheet of paper into the print engine along a path called the *paper train*. The paper train pulls the paper past an electrically charged wire that passes a static electrical charge to the paper. The charge may be either positive or negative, depending upon the design of the printer. For this example, we'll assume the charge is positive.

5 Where each point of light strikes the drum, it causes a negatively charged film—usually made of zinc oxide and other materials—on the surface of the drum to change its charge so that the dots have the same electrical charge as the sheet of paper. In this example, the light would change the charge from negative to positive. Each positive charge marks a dot that eventually will print black on paper. The areas of the drum that remain untouched by the laser beam retain their negative charge and result in white areas on the hard copy.

6 About halfway through the drum's rotation, the drum comes into contact with a bin that contains a black powder called *toner*. The toner in this example has a negative electrical charge—the opposite of the charges created on the drum by the laser beam. Because particles with opposite static charges attract each other, toner sticks to the drum in a pattern of small dots wherever the laser beam created a charge.

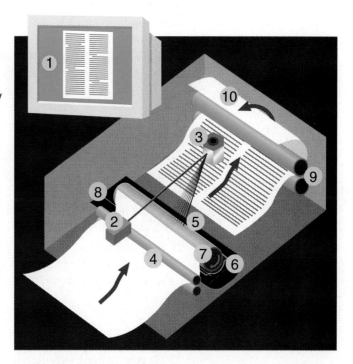

7 As the drum continues to turn, it presses against the sheet of paper being fed along the paper train. Although the electrical charge on the paper is the same as the charge of the drum created by the laser beam, the paper's charge is stronger and pulls the toner off the drum and onto the paper.

8 The rotation of the drum brings its surface next to a thin wire called the *corona wire*. It's called that because electricity passing through the wire creates a ring, or corona, around it that has a positive charge. The corona returns the entire surface of the drum to its original negative charge so that another page can be drawn on the drum's surface by the laser beam.

9 Another set of rollers pulls the paper through a part of the print engine called the *fusing system*. There pressure and heat bind the toner permanently to the paper by melting and pressing a wax that is part of the toner. The heat from the fusing system is what causes paper fresh from a laser printer to be warm.

10 The paper train pushes the paper out of the printer, usually with the printed side down so that pages end up in the output tray in the correct order.

FIGURE 11

Drum plotters

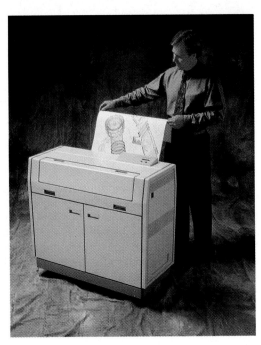

Monitors

"Softcopy" output is typically displayed on a monitor, a television-like screen on which you can read text and graphics. Monitors run under the control of a graphics display adapter card plugged into an expansion slot on the system board. The adapter allows information to leave the computer and appear on the monitor. The display adapter comes with its own RAM, called *VRAM*, or *video RAM*. VRAM controls the resolution of images displayed on the monitor, as well as the number of colors and the speed at which the images are displayed. In addition, the more video memory you have, the higher the resolution and the more colors you can display. A video display adapter with 1 megabyte of memory can support the display of 16.7 million colors.

The **cathode-ray tube (CRT)** is the most common type of monitor used with desktop computer systems; this technology is also used in standard TV sets. The CRT's screen display is made up of small picture elements (dots), called *pixels* for short. A **pixel** is the smallest unit on the screen that can be turned on or off or made to appear in different shades. A stream of bits defining the image is sent from the computer to the CRT's electron gun, where electrons are activated according to the bit patterns. *(See Figure 12.)* The inside of the front of the CRT screen is coated with phosphor. When a beam of electrons from the electron gun (deflected through a yoke) hits the phosphor, it lights up selected pixels to generate an image on the screen. A television monitor cannot be used directly with a display adapter since it cannot support the same number of pixels. (Television monitors support fewer but much larger pixels.) There are, however, converters that allow you to display a computer image on a standard TV monitor.

Flat-panel displays, which are much thinner, weigh less, and consume less power than CRTs, are used in portable computers. Experts predict that flat-panels will soon be used in desktop computers also, however the current problem is cost. A flat-panel display for a desktop microcomputer costs 4–8 times as much as an equivalent monitor based on CRT technology. The two types of flat-panel displays that you will likely encounter are the *liquid-crystal display (LCD)* and the *electroluminescent display (EL). (See Figure 13.)*

FIGURE 12	How a CRT works. *(Right)* A stream of bits from the computer's CPU is sent to the electron gun, which converts the bits into electrons. The gun then shoots a beam of electrons through the yoke, which deflects the beam in different directions. When the beam hits the phosphor coating on the inside of the CRT screen, a number of pixels light up, making the image on the screen. *(Left)* Each character on the screen is made up of small dots called *pixels*, short for *picture elements.*

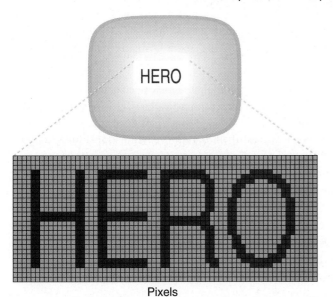

Pixels

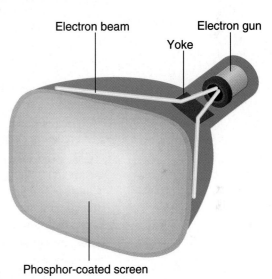

Electron beam

Electron gun

Yoke

Phosphor-coated screen

FIGURE 13

Flat-panel displays. *(Left)* Active matrix LCD, Planar System's CleanScreen compact computer for Hospital information systems. *(Right)* Planar EL screen.

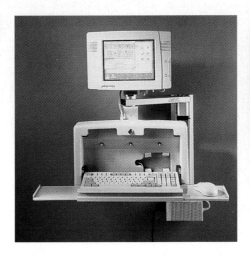

Whether for CRT or flat-panel, screen clarity depends on three qualities: *resolution, dot pitch,* and *refresh rate.*

- *Resolution:* The clarity or sharpness of a display screen, which is also dependent on the graphics display adapter, is called its **resolution;** the more pixels there are per square inch, the better the resolution. Resolution is expressed in terms of the formula *columns of pixels* $\times$ *rows of pixels.* Thus a screen with 640 $\times$ 480 pixels multiplied together equals 307,200 pixels. This screen will be less clear and sharp than screens with higher resolutions. Standard screen resolutions are 640 $\times$ 480, 800 $\times$ 600, 1024 $\times$ 768, 1280 $\times$ 1024, and 1600 $\times$ 1200. Some display adapters can handle all these resolutions, while others may go only as high as 1024 $\times$ 768. The display adapter also controls the number of colors that can be displayed at each resolution.

- *Dot pitch:* The *dot pitch* is the amount of space between pixels; the closer the dots, the crisper the image. A .28 dot pitch means dots are 28/100ths of a millimeter apart. Generally, a dot pitch of less than .31 will provide clear images. Multimedia and desktop publishing users typically employ .25 mm dot pitch monitors.

- *Refresh rate:* The *refresh rate* is the number of times per second that the pixels are recharged so that their glow remains bright. Refresh is necessary because the phosphors hold their glow for just a fraction of a second. The higher the refresh rate, the more solid the image looks on the screen—that is, it doesn't flicker. The refresh rate should be at least 70 Hz (Hertz).

The more colors and the higher the refresh rate and the resolution, the harder the display adapter has to work, and the more expensive it is. And the higher the settings, the slower the adapter operates. Also, for a display to work, video display adapters and monitors must be compatible. Your computer's software and the video display adapter must also be compatible. Thus, if your are changing your monitor or your video display adapter, be sure the new one will still work with the old.

Audio-Output Hardware

Another type of softcopy output is audio output, such as voice or music. **Voice-output devices** convert digital data into speech-like sounds. These devices are no longer very unusual. You hear such forms of voice output on telephones ("Please hang up and dial your call again"), in soft-drink machines, in cars, in toys and games, and recently in vehicle-navigation devices. **Sound-output devices** produce digitized sounds, ranging from beeps and chirps to music. All these sounds are nonverbal. PC owners can customize their machines to greet each new program with the sound of breaking glass or to moo like a cow every hour. To exercise these possibilities, you need both the necessary software and the sound card, or digital audio circuit board (such as SoundBlaster). The sound card plugs into an expansion slot in your computer, but it is commonly integrated with the motherboard on newer computers. A sound card is also required in making computerized music.

STORAGE HARDWARE

As previously mentioned, the function of *secondary storage hardware* is to provide a means of storing software and data in a form that is relatively permanent, or *non-volatile*—that is, the data is not lost when the power is turned off—and is easy to retrieve when needed for processing. Storage hardware serves the same basic functions as do office-filing systems except that it stores data as electromagnetic signals or laser-etched spots, commonly on magnetic disk, optical disk, or tape, rather than on paper.

As you learned, the data you are working on is stored in RAM (primary storage) in an electrical state during processing. Because RAM is an electrical state, when you turn off the power to your computer, data in RAM disappears. Therefore, before you turn your microcomputer off, you must save your work onto a storage device that stores data permanently (until it is erased)—such as a diskette or a hard disk. When saved to a secondary storage device, your data will remain intact even when the computer is turned off. Next, we describe some common storage devices.

Tape Storage

Magnetic tape used to be a routinely used secondary storage medium. However, these days, magnetic tape is used mainly on large systems for backup and archiving (maintaining historical records) and on some microcomputers for backup. **Cartridge tape units,** also called *tape streamers,* are commonly used with microcomputers to back up data from a hard disk onto a tape cartridge. *(See Figure 14.)*

FIGURE 14

Cartridge tape units are often used with microcomputers to back up data from a hard disk.

Internal tape drive with tape cassette

External tape drive

" 'When you lose a disk, you're not only losing the hardware and software,' said John L. Copen, president of Integ, an information protection company in Manhattan. 'The information has to be reproduced, and if you have to reproduce it without a backup...'

Mr. Copen demonstrates the point by holding up a digital audio-tape (DAT) cassette, . . . used for backing up data on larger hard disk drives, the kind that act as hubs for networks of personal computers in an office.

'I ask people in the audience what it's worth,' he said. 'It's a little cassette about the size of a credit card. The cassette costs about $16. I ask them to guess how much it can store. Forty megs? Eighty megs? It stores four gigabytes.' A gigabyte is roughly a thousand megabytes, or a billion characters of information.

'How much information can you put in four gigs?' Mr. Copen continued. 'About 20,000 big spreadsheets, which translates to about 100,000 days of work, or 800,000 hours. At $20 an hour, that's $16 million. Never before have people been able to reach down, pick up a cassette and walk out the door with $16 million of data in their pocket.' "

— Peter H. Lewis, "Finding an Electronic Safe-Deposit Data Box," *New York Times*

A cartridge tape unit using ¼-inch cassettes (QIC, or Quarter-Inch Cartridge standard) fits into a standard slot in the microcomputer system cabinet and uses mini-cartridges that can store gigabytes of data on a single tape. A more advanced form of cassette, adapted from technology used in the music industry, is the digital audio tape (DAT), which uses 2- or 3-inch cassettes and stores 2–4 GB. Redesigned DATs called Travan technology are expected to hold as much as 8 gigabytes.

Diskette Storage

A **diskette,** or *floppy disk,* is a removable round, flat piece of mylar plastic that stores data and programs, as tape does, as magnetized spots. More specifically, data is stored as electromagnetic charges on a metal oxide film that coats the mylar plastic. Data is represented by the presence or absence of these electromagnetic charges, following standard patterns of data representation (such as ASCII). The diskette is contained in a square plastic case to protect it from being touched. Diskettes are often called "floppy" because the disk within the case is flexible, not rigid. The most common size of diskette is 3½ inches in diameter. *(See Figure 15.)*

FIGURE 15

Diskettes

There are a number of rules for taking care of diskettes. In general, they boil down to the following:

- *Don't touch diskette surfaces:* Don't touch anything visible through the protective case.

- *Handle diskettes gently:* Don't bend them or put anything of weight upon them.

- *Avoid risky physical environments:* Keep diskettes out of the direct sunlight and heat. Also, they should not be placed near magnetic fields (including those created by nearby telephones or stereos).

To use a diskette, you need a **disk drive.** A disk drive is a device that holds, spins, and reads data from and writes data to the diskette. In the context of secondary storage, the words *read* and *write* have exact meanings. **Read** means that the data represented by the magnetized spots on the disk (or tape) is converted to electronic signals and transmitted to primary storage (RAM) in the computer. That, read means that data is copied from the diskette. **Write** means that the electronic information processed by the computer is recorded onto disk (or tape). Data, represented as electronic signals within the computer's memory, is transferred onto the disk (tape) and is then stored as magnetized stops. The diskette drive (floppy drive) is usually housed inside the computer's system cabinet.

How a Disk Drive Works

A diskette is inserted into a slot, called the drive gate or drive door, in the front of the disk drive. *(See Figure 16.)* This clamps the diskette in place over the spindle of the drive mechanism so that drive can operate. An access light goes on when the disk is in use. After using the disk, you remove it by pressing an eject button beside the drive. *(Note:* Do not eject the disk when the access light is on!)

The device by which the data on a disk is transferred to the computer, and from the computer to the disk, is the disk drive's read/write head. The diskette spins inside its case, and the read/write head moves back and forth over the data access area, which is under the diskette's metal protective plate. This plate slides aside when you insert the diskette into the drive.

Diskettes have the following characteristics:

- *Tracks and sectors:* On a diskette, data is recorded in rings called *tracks,* which are neither visible grooves nor a single spiral. Rather, they are closed concentric rings. *(See Figure 17.)* The number of tracks on a diskette is referred to as *TPI,* or *tracks per inch.* The higher the TPI, the more data the diskette can hold. Most diskettes are 135 TPI.

    Each track is divided into sectors. Sectors are invisible pie- or wedge-shaped sections used by the computer for storage reference purposes. The number of sectors on the diskette varies according to the recording density—the number of bits per inch. Each sector typically holds 512 bytes of data. When you save data from your computer to a diskette, it is distributed by tracks and sectors on the disk. That is, the systems software uses the point at which a sector intersects a track to reference the data location in order to spin the disk and position the read/write head.

- *Unformatted versus formatted diskettes:* When you buy a new box of diskettes, the box may state that they are "formatted." However, if they are not formatted, you have a task to perform before you can use the disks with

FIGURE 16

Cutaway view of a diskette drive

When a diskette is inserted into the drive, it presses against a system of levers. One lever opens the metal plate, or shutter, to expose the data access area.

Other levers and gears move two read/write heads until they almost touch the diskette on both sides.

The drive's circuit board receives signals, including data and instructions for reading/ writing that data from/to disk, from the drive's controller board. The circuit board translates the instructions into signals that control the movement of the disk and the read/write heads.

A motor located beneath the disk spins a shaft that engages a notch on the hub of the disk, causing the disk to spin.

When the heads are in the correct position, electrical impulses create a magnetic field in one of the heads to write data to either the top or bottom surface of the disk. When the heads are reading data, they react to magnetic fields generated by the metallic particles on the disk.

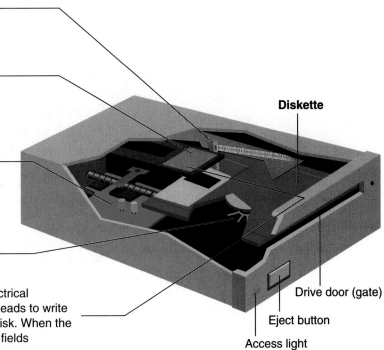

Diskette

Drive door (gate)

Eject button

Access light

3½-inch diskette

Front

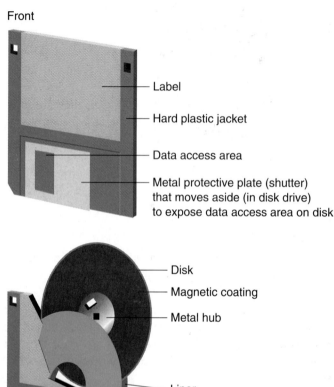

— Label

— Hard plastic jacket

— Data access area

— Metal protective plate (shutter)
that moves aside (in disk drive)
to expose data access area on disk

— Disk

— Magnetic coating

— Metal hub

— Liner

— Shell

— Shutter

Back

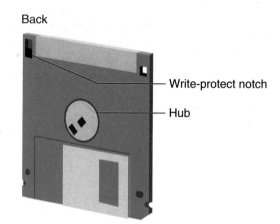

— Write-protect notch

— Hub

**Tracks
and
Sectors**

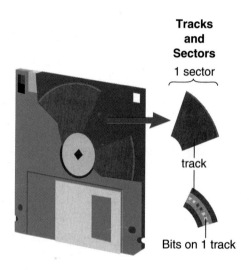

1 sector

track

Bits on 1 track

FIGURE 17

Parts of a diskette

your computer and disk drive. Unformatted disks are manufactured without tracks and sectors in place. **Formatting**—or **initializing,** as it is called on the Macintosh—means that you must prepare the disk for use so that the computer's operating systems software can write information on it. This includes defining the tracks and sectors on it.

The software documentation that comes with your microcomputer tells you what commands to enter to format your diskettes. It is important to note that if you ever reformat a disk with data already written to it, *all* data will be lost during the reformatting process.

- *Write-protect features:* Diskettes have features to prevent someone from accidentally writing over—and thereby obliterating—data on the diskette or making changes to program files. To write-protect your diskette, you press a lever toward the edge of the diskette, uncovering a hole (which appears on the lower right side, viewed from the back). *(See Figure 18.)*

Writable

Write-protected

Write-protect
window closed

Write-protect
window open

FIGURE 18

Write-protect features. For data to be written to this disk, a small piece of plastic must be pushed over the tiny window on one side of the disk. To protect the disk from being written to, you must open the window (using the tip of a pen helps).

Hard Disks

Comparing the use of diskettes to hard disks is like discovering the difference between moving your household in several trips in a small sportscar and doing it all at once with a moving van. Whereas a high-density 3½ inch diskette holds 1.44 megabytes of data, a hard disk in a personal computer may hold up to 9 gigabytes. Indeed, at first, with a hard disk you may feel you have more storage capacity than you'll ever need. However, after a few months, you may begin to worry that you don't have enough. This feeling may be intensified if you're using multimedia or graphics-oriented programs with digital video and graphic-intensive data requiring immense amounts of storage.

Diskettes are made out of flexible material, which makes them "floppy." By contrast, **hard disks** are thin but rigid metal or glass platters covered with a substance that allows data to be held in the form of magnetized spots. Hard disks are also tightly sealed within an enclosed unit to prevent any foreign matter—dust or smoke, for example—from getting inside. Data may be recorded on both sides of the disk platters. (*See Figure 19.*) The disks may be 5¼ inches in diameter, although today they are more often 1–3½ inches. The operation is much the same as for a diskette drive, with the read/write heads locating specific pieces of data according to track, sector, and disk surface number. Whereas diskettes usually have 135 tracks per inch (TPI), hard disks have thousands; whereas an HD diskette may have 18 sectors, a hard disk may have up to 64.

We mentioned that hard disks have a data storage capacity that is significantly greater than that of diskettes. Microcomputer hard disk drives now typically hold 2–4 gigabytes. As for speed, hard disks allow faster access to data than do diskettes because a hard disk spins several times faster than a diskette.

Optical Disks

An **optical disk** is a removable disk on which data is written and read through the use of laser beams: There is no mechanical arm, as with diskettes and hard disks. The most familiar form of optical disk is the one used in the music industry. A compact disk, or CD, is an audio disk using digital code that is like a miniature phonograph record. A CD holds up to 74 minutes (2 billion bits' worth) of high-fidelity stereo sound.

FIGURE 19   Microcomputer internal hard disk drive

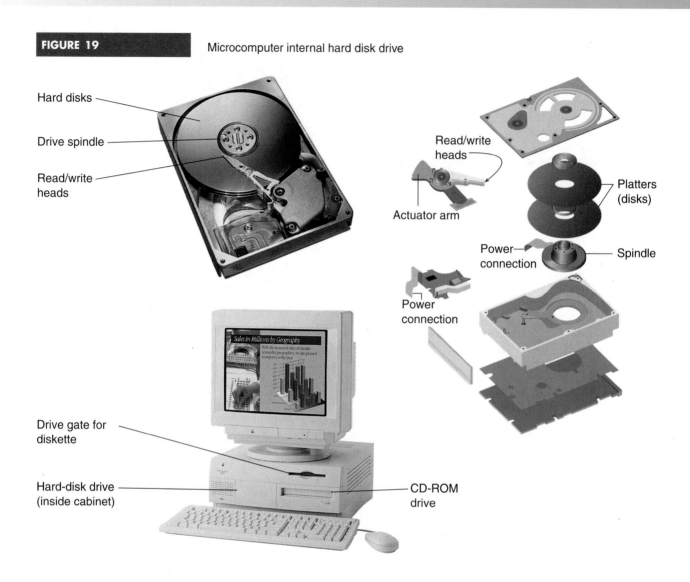

The optical disk technology that revolutionized the music business with music CDs has done the same for secondary storage with computers. A single optical disk of the type called CD-ROM may hold 680 megabytes of data. This works out to 250,000 pages of text, or more than 7,000 photos or graphics, or 19 hours of speech, or 74 minutes of video. Although some disks are used strictly for digital data storage, many are used to distribute multimedia programs that combine text, visuals, and sound.

In the principal types of optical disk technology, a high-power laser beam is used to represent data by burning tiny pits into the surface of a hard-plastic disk. To read the data, a low-powered laser light scans the disk surface: Pitted areas are not reflected and are interpreted as 0 bits; smooth areas are reflected and are interpreted as 1 bits. *(See Figure 20.)* Because the pits are so tiny, a great deal more data can be represented than is possible in the same amount of space on a diskette and many hard disks. CD-ROMS have enabled the development of the multimedia business. *Multimedia* refers to technology that presents information in more than one medium, including text, graphics, animation, video, sound, and voice.

FIGURE 20

Optical disks. *(Top)* Writing data: A high-powered laser beam records data by burning tiny pits onto the disk's surface. *(Bottom)* Reading data: A low-powered laser beam reads data by reflecting smooth areas, which are interpreted as 1 bits, and not reflecting pitted areas, which are interpreted as 0 bits.

Recording data

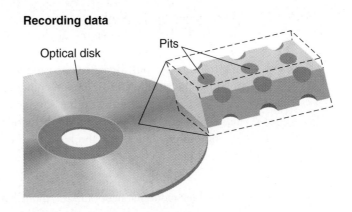

Reading data

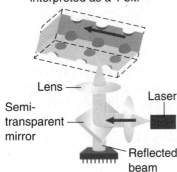

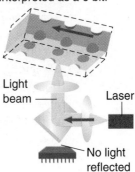

COMMUNICATIONS HARDWARE

The function of **communications hardware** is to facilitate the connections between computers and between groups of connected computers called *networks*. Of course, computers can be "stand-alone" machines, meaning that they are not connected to anything else. Indeed many students tote around portable microcomputers that they user for word processing and other programs. However, the communications component of a computer system vastly extends the computer's range and utility.

In general, computer communications is of two types: wired connections, such as telephone wire and cable, and wireless connections, such as microwaves, satellites, and radio waves. Because the dominant communications media that have been developed during this century use analog transmission, the principal form of direct connection has been via standard copper-wire telephone lines. Hundreds of these copper wires are bundled together in cables strung in telephone poles or buried underground.

As we mentioned earlier, a *modem* converts digital signals into analog form to send over phone lines. A receiving modem at the other end of the phone line then converts the analog signal back to a digital signal. *(See Figure 21.)* Modems are either internal or external. Because most modems use standard telephone lines, users are charged the usual rates by phone companies, whether local or long-distance. Users are also often charged by online services for time spent online. Accordingly, *transmission speed,* the speed at which modems transmit data, becomes an important consideration. The faster the modem, the less time you need to spend on the telephone line.

With older modems, users talked about *baud rate,* the speed at which data is transmitted, measured by the number of times per second the signal being transmitted changes. At lower speeds, one bit was usually transmitted with each signal change per second—thus the baud rate could be the same as the bits-per-second (bps) rate. Baud rate applied to very slow speeds (such as 300 bps, the speed of a modem 15 years ago). At speeds above 2400 bps, more than 1 bit is transmitted with each signal change; thus today users refer to *bits per second (bps)* or, more likely, *kilobits per second (Kbps)* to express data transmission speeds. A 28,800-bps modem, for example, is a 28.8-Kpbs modem. Old modems transmitted at 1200, 2400, 4800, and 9600 bps (slow and not worth using anymore). Newer modems operate at 14,400 and 28,800 bps (moderately fast) and 33,600 and 56,000 bps (high-speed). A 10-page single-spaced letter can be transmitted by a 2400-bps modem in 2½ minutes. It can be transmitted by a 28,800-bps modem in about 10 seconds, and by a 56,000-bps modem in about 5 seconds. (Currently there are two incompatible types of 56 Kbps modems; however, a single standard is expected to evolve shortly.)

QUICK CHECK   **Could a computer work without main memory? Why or why not?**

Explain the difference between primary storage and secondary storage.

Inside the Microcomputer

As we mentioned earlier, the case or cabinet that contains the microcomputer's processing hardware and other components is called the **system unit.** *(See Figure 22.)* The system unit does not typically include the monitor, keyboard, or printer. It usually does include a hard-disk drive, a diskette drive, a CD-ROM

FIGURE 21

A sending modem translates digital signals into analog waves for transmission over phone lines. A receiving modem translates the analog signals back into digital signals.

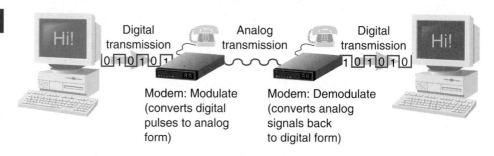

Digital transmission 010101

Analog transmission

Digital transmission 101010

Modem: Modulate (converts digital pulses to analog form)

Modem: Demodulate (converts analog signals back to digital form)

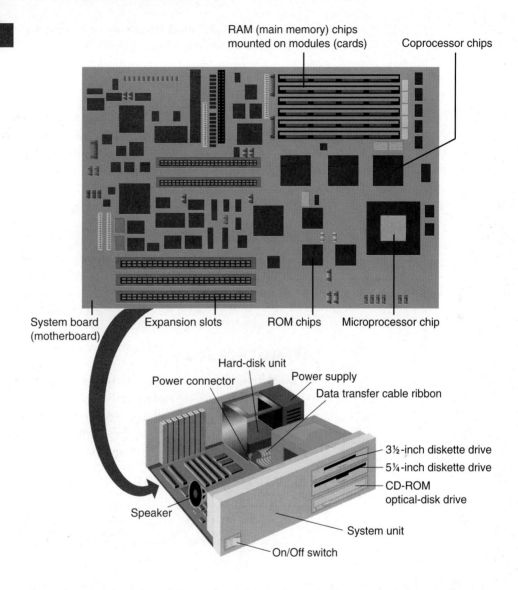

FIGURE 22

The system unit and its contents

RAM (main memory) chips mounted on modules (cards)

Coprocessor chips

System board (motherboard)

Expansion slots

ROM chips

Microprocessor chip

Hard-disk unit

Power connector

Power supply

Data transfer cable ribbon

3½-inch diskette drive

5¼-inch diskette drive

CD-ROM optical-disk drive

Speaker

System unit

On/Off switch

drive, and sometimes a tape drive. We described these secondary storage devices and other peripheral devices in the previous sections. Here we are concerned with the following parts of the system unit:

- Power supply
- Motherboard
- Microprocessor
- RAM chips
- ROM chips
- Other forms of memory
- Ports
- Expansion slots and boards
- Bus lines and PC slots and cards

1. control signal
2. address
3. data

These are terms that appear frequently in advertisements for microcomputers. After reading this section, you should be able to understand what these ads are talking about.

THE POWER SUPPLY

The electricity available from a standard wall outlet is AC (alternating current), but a microcomputer runs on DC (direct current). The power supply is the device that converts power from AC to DC to run the computer. The on/off switch in your computer turns on or shuts off the electricity to the power supply. Because electricity can generate a lot of heat, a fan inside the computer keeps the power supply and other components from becoming too hot.

Electrical power drawn from a standard AC outlet can be quite uneven. A sudden surge, or "spike," in AC voltage can burn out the low-voltage DC circuitry in your computer ("fry the motherboard"). Instead of plugging your computer directly into the wall electrical outlet, it's a good idea to plug it into a power protection device, which is in turn plugged into the wall outlet. The two principal types are *surge protectors* and *UPS (uninterruptable power supply) units.*

THE MOTHERBOARD

The **motherboard,** also called the *system board,* is the main circuit board in the system unit. The motherboard consists of a flat board that contains the microprocessor, any coprocessor chips, RAM chips, ROM chips, some other types of memory, and *expansion slots,* where additional circuit boards, called *expansion boards,* may be plugged in. *(Refer back to Figure 22.)*

THE MICROPROCESSOR

Most microcomputers today use microprocessors of two kinds, those made by Intel and those by Motorola. About 90% of microcomputers use Intel-type microprocessors; thus most applications software packages have been written for Intel platforms.

- *Intel chips:* Intel makes chips for IBM and IBM-compatible computers such as Compaq, Dell, Gateway and Toshiba. Variations of Intel chips are made by other companies, such as Advanced Micro Devices (AMD), Cyrix Inc., and Chips and Technologies. Intel used to identify its chips by numbers—8086, 8088, 80286, 80386, 80486: the "x86" series. Intel's successor to the x86 chips is the Pentium family of chips—the *Pentium, Pentium Pro, Pentium MMX,* and *Pentium II.* In the 1970s a microprocessor may have had about 2300 transistors and run at only 1 MHz; now some microprocessors have more than 5.5 million transistors and run faster than 300 MHz.

- *Motorola chips:* Motorola makes chips for Apple Macintosh computers. These chip numbers include the 68000, 68020, 68030, and 68040. More recently, Motorola joined forces with IBM and Apple and produced the PowerPC family of chips. With some software and/or hardware add-ons, a Power PC can run applications software written for *both* Apple and IBM platforms.

RAM CHIPS

As we described earlier in the chapter, *main memory,* or *RAM (random access memory),* is memory that temporarily holds data and instructions that will be needed shortly by the processor. RAM operates like a chalkboard that is constantly being written on, then erased, then written on again.

Like the microprocessor, RAM is made up of circuit-inscribed silicon chips. Microcomputers come with different amounts of RAM. In many cases, additional RAM chips can be added by plugging a memory-expansion card into the system board. In most cases, the more RAM you have, the faster the software can operate. If, for instance, you type such a long document in a word processing program that it will not all fit into your computer's RAM, the computer will put part of the document onto your disk (either hard disk or diskette). This *disk caching* process means you have to wait while the computer swaps data back and forth between RAM and disk. Microcomputer users need 16–32 MB or more of RAM to run today's popular software.

Having enough RAM has become a critical matter! Before you buy any software package, look at the outside of the box to see how much RAM is required to run it by itself and to run it at the same time as other programs you commonly use.

ROM CHIPS

Unlike RAM, which is constantly being written on and erased, **ROM,** which stands for **read-only memory** and is also known as *firmware,* cannot be written on or erased (without special equipment) by the computer user. (Firmware is a term used for software permanently stored on a chip.) In other words, RAM chips remember, temporarily, information supplied by you or a software program; ROM chips remember, permanently, information supplied by the manufacturer.

One of the ROM chips contains instructions that tell the processor what to do when you first turn on, or "boot" the computer. These instructions are called the *ROM bootstrap,* because they get the computer system going by helping to "pull itself up by its bootstraps" and by performing a "power-on self-test" (POST). Another ROM chip helps the processor transfer information between the keyboard, screen, printer, and other peripheral devices to make sure all units are functioning properly. These instructions are called ROM BIOS, or basic input/output system. Fundamentally, ROM BIOS is an interface, a connector, and a translator between the computer hardware and the software programs that you run.

OTHER FORMS OF MEMORY

In addition to inserting SIMMs in expansion slots, as we mentioned earlier, adding other forms of memory can enhance a microcomputer's performance, as follows:

- *Cache memory:* In the most powerful computers and in high-end microcomputers, RAM is divided into two sections. One section is relatively large (several rows of chips) and is called *main RAM.* The other section is tiny, just a few chips. This cache (pronounced "cash") memory, which typically

Diagram of cache memory
operation

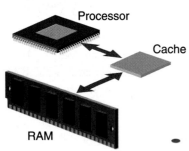

Processor

Cache

RAM

amounts to 256 K or 512 K, is much faster but also much more expensive than RAM. **Cache memory** is a special high-speed memory area that the processor can access quickly. Essentially, cache memory is a bridge between the processor and RAM. *(See Figure 23.)* A special "look-ahead program" transfers the data and instructions that were transferred from secondary storage to RAM from RAM to the processor. This allows the processor to run faster because it doesn't have to take time to swap instructions in and out of RAM. There are several types of cache memory available. One type you see advertised frequently in computer magazine ads is *pipeline-burst cache,* which allows memory chips to be read from and written to at the same time.

- *Video memory:* Video memory chips. such as *video RAM (VRAM), WRAM,* and *SGRAM,* are used to store display images for the monitor. The amount of video memory determines how fast images appear and how many colors are available at specific resolutions. Video memory chips are particularly desirable if you are running programs that display a lot of graphics. These chips are usually located on a special video adapter card inserted in an expansion slot on the system board.

- *Flash memory:* Used primarily in portable computers, **flash memory,** or **flash RAM cards,** consist of circuitry on credit card-size cards that can be inserted into slots connecting to the system board. Unlike standard RAM chips, flash memory is *nonvolatile.* That is, it retains data even when the power is turned off. Flash memory can be used not only to simulate main memory but also to supplement or replace hard disk drives for permanent storage. Some experts predict that flash RAM will eventually replace traditional RAM.

PORTS: CONNECTING PERIPHERALS

Microcomputers have different types of ports, depending on whether they use the PC or the Mac platform and how recent the model is. A **port** is a socket on the outside of the system unit that is connected by a bus to an expansion board on the inside of the system unit or connected directly to integrated circuitry on the motherboard. A port allows you to use a cable to plug in a peripheral device, such as a monitor, printer, or modem, so that it can communicate with the computer system.

Ports are of several types *(see Figure 24):*

- A *parallel port,* often labeled "LPT" on the back of a PC, allows 8 bits of data to be transmitted simultaneously, like cars moving in the same direction on an eight-lane highway. Parallel lines move information faster than serial lines do, but they can transmit information efficiently only up to 15 feet. Thus, parallel ports are used principally for connecting printers and external storage devices.

- A *serial port,* or *RS-232 port,* enables a line to be connected that will send bits one after the other on a single line, like cars on a one-lane highway. Serial lines are used to link equipment that is not close by. Serial ports are

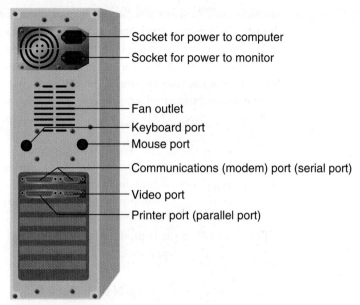

FIGURE 24

Some typical microcomputer ports

Socket for power to computer
Socket for power to monitor
Fan outlet
Keyboard port
Mouse port
Communications (modem) port (serial port)
Video port
Printer port (parallel port)

IBM-compatible

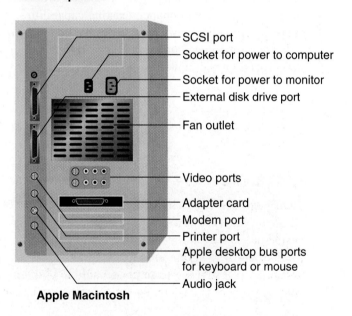

SCSI port
Socket for power to computer
Socket for power to monitor
External disk drive port
Fan outlet
Video ports
Adapter card
Modem port
Printer port
Apple desktop bus ports for keyboard or mouse
Audio jack

Apple Macintosh

used principally for communications lines, modems, and mice and, in the case of the Macintosh, the printer. (Serial ports are often called "COM" ports, for communications.) On the back of most PCs can be found one 9-pin connector for serial port COM1, typically used for the mouse, and one 25-pin connector for serial port COM 2, typically used for the modem.

● *Video adapter ports* are used to connect the video display monitor outside the computer to the video adapter card inside the system unit. Monitors may have either a 9-pin plug or a 25-pin plug. The plug must be compatible with the number of holes in the video adapter card.

- A *SCSI port,* pronounced "scuzzy" (and short for Small Computer System Interface), provides an interface for transferring data at high speeds for up to seven or fifteen SCSI-compatible devices, linked together in what is called a *daisy chain,* along an extended cable. (*See Figure 25.*) These devices include internal and external hard disk drives, CD-ROM drives, tape backup units, and scanners.

- *Games* and *MIDI ports* allow you to attach a joystick, game-playing device, or musical instrument to the system.

- Wireless, *infrared* (*IR*) data-transfer ports are available on new computers and hardware peripherals such as printers. This type of connection uses a certain frequency of radio waves to transmit data, so it requires an unobstructed line of sight between the transmitter and the receiver. Most new laptop and notebook computers provide IR ports for linking directly to desktop computers and printers.

EXPANSION SLOTS AND BOARDS

Most of today's microcomputers have *open architecture*—that is, users can easily add new devices and enhance existing capabilities. This spares users from having to buy a completely new computer every time they want to upgrade something. As with ports, microcomputers will have different numbers and kinds of expansion slots, based on the model.

FIGURE 25

Daisy chains

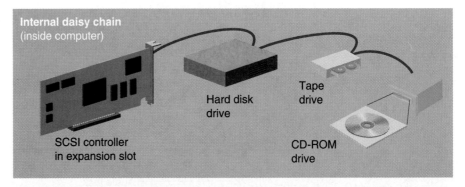

Internal daisy chain (inside computer)

Hard disk drive
Tape drive
SCSI controller in expansion slot
CD-ROM drive

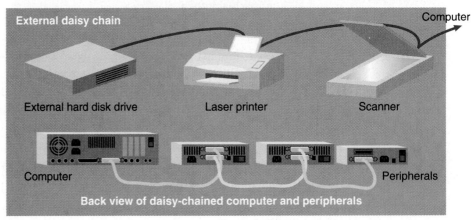

External daisy chain
Computer

External hard disk drive
Laser printer
Scanner

Computer
Peripherals

Back view of daisy-chained computer and peripherals

Expansion slots are sockets on the system board into which you can plug expansion cards. *(Refer back to Figure 22.)* These sockets connect to buses. **Expansion cards,** or *add-on boards,* are circuit boards that provide networking capabilities, communications, sound and video capabilities, or control peripheral devices. The words *card* and *board* are used interchangeably. Some slots will be needed right away for ordinary peripherals, but if you have enough free slots open, you can use them for expansion later. (*Note:* Each kind of expansion card is designed to work with a particular expansion bus.)

BUSES

As we mentioned earlier, a **bus** line, or simply bus, is a hardware pathway through which bits are transmitted within the processor and between the processor and other devices in the system unit. The computer's internal bus is known as the *local bus,* or *processor bus.* Other types of buses, called *expansion buses,* connect various types of peripheral devices to the computer via connection to expansion cards inserted in the system board.

A computer bus provides parallel data transfer. For example, a 16-bit bus (for example, the ISA standard) transfers 2 bytes (16 bites) at a time over 16 wires; a 32-bit bus (for example, the PCI standard) transmits 4 bytes (32 bits) at a time over 32 wires, and so on. Today there are several standard bus designs, or architectures. When buying a new system or expanding an existing one, you need to check that cards and peripherals are compatible with the types of buses you have.

QUICK CHECK   **What's the difference between RAM and ROM?**

COMPUTER SOFTWARE

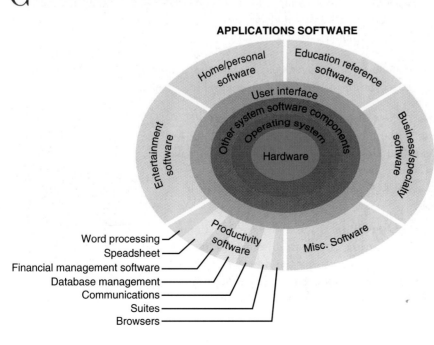

APPLICATIONS SOFTWARE

Home/personal software

Education reference software

User interface

Other system software components

Operating system

Hardware

Entertainment software

Business/specialty software

Word processing
Spreadsheet
Financial management software
Database management
Communications
Suites
Browsers

Productivity software

Misc. Software

Software consists of the step-by-step instructions that tell the computer how to perform a task. Software is "soft" because you cannot touch the instructions the way that you can touch the computer equipment—the "hard" ware. There are two basic types of software: system software, for the computer, and applications software, for the user. Software consists of programs (instructions), not data. Thus software is "run," whereas data is "processed."

Every application works through "layers" in the computer to get to the hardware and perform the desired result. Think of the applications software layer as what the computer is doing and the system software as how the computer does it.

Software is made up of a group of related *programs* written in a specific code called a *programming language* and based on the computer's language of 0s and 1s. In turn, each program is made up of a group of related instructions that perform specific processing tasks. Software acquired to perform a general business function is often referred to as a *software package.* Software is usually created by professional software programmers and comes on disk, CD-ROM, or online, across the Internet.

SYSTEM SOFTWARE: THE COMPUTER'S BOSS

Software designed to allow the computer to manage its own resources and run basic operations is called **system software.** This software runs the basic operations: It lets the CPU communicate with the keyboard, the screen, the printer, and the disk drive. However, it does not solve specific problems relating to a business or a profession.

System software is automatically loaded into your computer's memory (RAM) when you turn the computer on. This process is called **booting.** Most systems software uses a **graphical user interface (GUI),** which uses graphics to help the user recognize functions and resources. *(See Figure 26.)*

Examples of systems software are DOS, Windows 95, Windows NT, OS/2, Macintosh Operating System, and Unix.

APPLICATIONS SOFTWARE: YOUR SERVANT

Applications software allows you to increase your productivity and creativity in ways simply not possible without it. **Applications software** is software that performs tasks to directly benefit or assist the user.

Ready-made applications software can be purchased "off the shelf" from a computer store or a mail-order supplier, or it can be created, or customized, to specification by a programmer.

Most applications software packages share similar features and functions, many of which are based on the system software's graphical user interface.

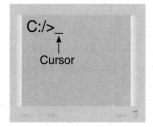

C:/>
Cursor

- *Cursor:* The **cursor,** also called the *insertion point,* is the movable symbol on the display screen that shows you where you may enter data next. You can move the cursor around using either the keyboard's directional arrow keys or a mouse.

- *Scrolling;* **Scrolling** is the activity of moving quickly upward or downward through the text or other screen display using the directional arrow keys or a mouse. (*Note:* The term *panning* is used to describe the process of scrolling to the right and left.)

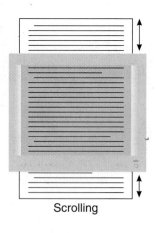

Scrolling

FIGURE 26   Windows 95 screen: graphical user interface

Start button: Click for an easy way to start using the computer.

Microsoft Network: Click here to connect to the Microsoft Network, the company's online service.

My Briefcase: Allows you to synchronize files between two computers—say, an office PC and a laptop.

Recycle Bin: Allows you to dispose of files—or retrieve them later.

Network Neighborhood: If your PC is linked to a network of PCs, click here to get a glimpse of everything available on the network.

My Computer: Gives you a quick overview of all the files and programs installed in your PC.

Document: Multitasking capabilities allow you to smoothly run more than one program at once.

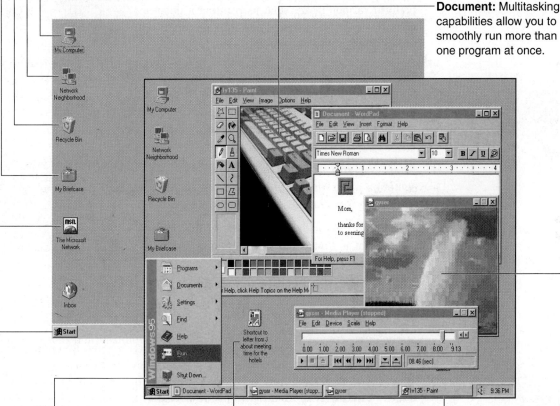

Start menu: After clicking on the Start button, a menu appears, giving you a quick way to handle common tasks. You can launch programs, call up documents, change system settings, get help, find files, and shut down your PC.

Shortcuts: Allows you to immediately launch often-used files and programs.

Taskbar: Gives you a log of all programs you have opened. To switch programs, click on the buttons that appear in the taskbar.

Multimedia: Windows 95 features improved audio, video, and graphics display capabilities.

Pull-down menu

Button on Toolbar

- *Windows:* A **window** is a rectangular section of the display screen with a title bar on top. Each window may display a different applications program or document.

- *Menu bar:* A **menu bar** is a row of menu options displayed across the top or the bottom of the screen.

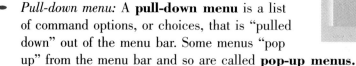

Menu bar

- *Pull-down menu:* A **pull-down menu** is a list of command options, or choices, that is "pulled down" out of the menu bar. Some menus "pop up" from the menu bar and so are called **pop-up menus.**

- *Help window:* A **Help window** offers a choice of *Help screens,* specific explanations on how to perform various tasks, such as printing a document. Help features include searchable topic indexes and online glossaries.

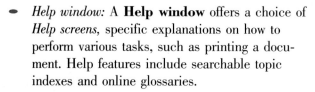

Help may also be available in the form of an assistant or a cartoon-like **wizard.** In this case, the applications program leads you through a series of questions to determine exactly what you need help with. Then it leads you through the steps to accomplish your objective.

- *Icons:* An **icon** is an on-screen pictorial representation of an object (file, program, disk, and so on) used in graphical user interfaces (GUIs).

- *Buttons:* A **button** is a simulated button on screen that is "pushed" by positioning the pointer on top of it and clicking the mouse. Pushing a button can execute a command.

- *Toolbars:* A **toolbar** is a row of on-screen buttons, usually appearing immediately below the menu bar, used to activate a variety of functions of the applications program. Toolbars can often be customized and moved around on the screen.

- *Dialog box:* A **dialog box** is a window or box that appears on the screen. It is used to collect information from the user and to display helpful messages.

Save changes?
yes no cancel

Dialog box

- *Default values:* **Default values** are the standard settings used by the computer when the user does not specify an alternative. For example, unless you specify particular margin widths in your Page setup settings, the word processing program will use the manufacturer's default values.

- *Macros:* A **macro** is a feature that allows you to use a single keystroke, command, or toolbar button to automatically issue a predetermined series of commands. Thus, you can consolidate several keystrokes or menu selections into only one or two keystrokes.

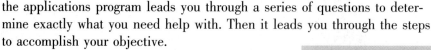

- *Clipboard:* Many applications software programs allow you to copy an item from one document and then paste it into another document or application—or copy an item and place the copy in another part of the same document. The **Clipboard** is the area is memory where the copy is held before it is pasted. (The Clipboard can hold only one item in memory at a time.)

- *Tutorials and documentation:* How are you going to learn the features available in a given software program? Most commercial packages come with tutorials. A **tutorial** is an instruction book or program that takes you through a prescribed series of steps to help you learn the product.

  Tutorials must be contrasted with documentation. **Documentation,** as we mentioned earlier, is a user manual or reference manual that is a narrative and graphical description of a program. Documentation may be instructional, but features and functions are usually grouped by category for reference purposes. For example, in word processing documentation, all cut-and-paste features are grouped together so you can easily look them up if you have forgotten how to perform them. Documentation may come in booklet form or on diskette or CD-ROM; it may also be available online from the manufacturer.

Many types of applications software are on the market. Some of the most common ones used today are word processing, spreadsheet, graphics, database management, communications, and electronic mail software.

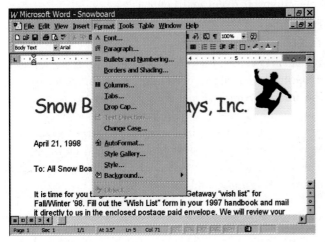

Word Processing

Word processing software allows you to use computers to create, edit, revise, store, and print many types of documents. It enables the user to easily insert, delete, and move words, sentences, and paragraphs—without ever using an eraser. Word processing programs also offer a number of features for "dressing up" documents with variable margins, type sizes, and styles. The user can do all these manipulations on screen, in "WYSIWYG" fashion, before printing out hardcopy. (WYSIWYG stands for "what you see is what you get," meaning that the screen displays documents exactly as they will look when printed.) Popular word processing programs are Microsoft Word and Corel's WordPerfect.

Spreadsheet

What is a spreadsheet? Traditionally, it was simply a grid of rows and columns, printed on special green paper that was used by accountants and others to produce financial reports. A person making up a spreadsheet often spent long days and weekends at the office penciling tiny numbers into countless tiny rectangles. When one figure changed, all the rest of the numbers on the spreadsheet had to be recomputed—ultimately there might be wastebaskets full of jettisoned worksheets. Spreadsheet software has changed this tedious process into a relatively easy one.

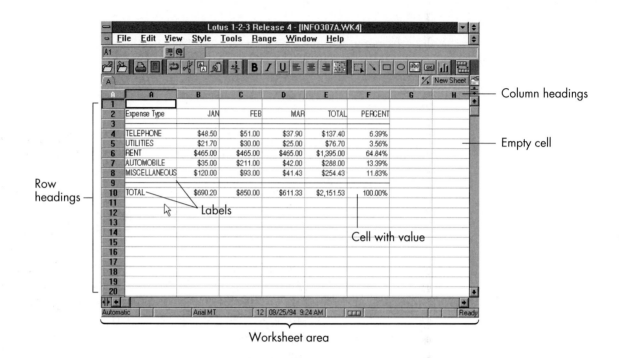

An electronic **spreadsheet** allows users to create tables and financial schedules by entering data into rows and columns arranged as a grid on a display screen. Today the principal spreadsheets are Microsoft Excel and Lotus 1-2-3.

Graphics

Using spreadsheet software, you can easily create analytical graphics called *charts*. These business graphics make numeric data easier to analyze than when it is in the form of rows and columns of numbers, as in electronic spreadsheets. Whether viewed on a monitor or printed out, charts help make sales figures, economic trends, and the like easier to comprehend and analyze. The principal examples of analytical graphics are *bar charts, line graphs,* and *pie charts.*

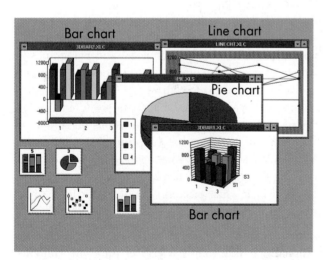

Creative graphics, such as commercial logos, advertising features, and artistic renderings are easily created, modified, and sent to press, film, or video. These computer graphics can also be manipulated for use in television and film, multimedia productions, and Web pages. Some examples of popular graphics software includes Adobe Photoshop, Adobe Illustrator, CorelDRAW, and 3D Studio Max.

Presentation graphics are more complex than analytical graphics. They are a feature of *presentation software,* which uses graphics and data/information from other software tools to communicate or make a presentation to others, such as clients or supervisors. Presentations may make use of some analytical graphics—bar, line, and pie charts—but they usually look much more sophisticated using, for instance, different texturing patterns (speckled, solid, cross-hatched), color, and three-dimensionality. The most well-known presentation software packages are Microsoft PowerPoint, Lotus Freelance Graphics, and SPC Harvard Graphics.

Database Management

In its most general sense, a database is any electronically stored collection of data in a computer system. In its more specific sense, a *database* is a collection of interrelated files in a computer system. These computer-based files are organized according to their common elements so that they can be retrieved easily. Sometimes called a *database manager* or *database management system (DBMS),* **database software** is a program that controls the structure of a database and access to the data. It allows the user to enter queries and to search for data, as well as to print out formatted reports.

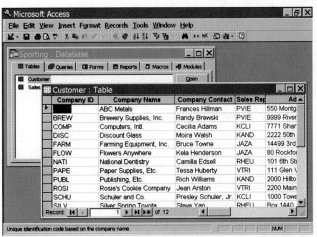

Databases are a lot more interesting than they used to be. Once they included only text. Digital technology has added new kinds of information—not only word processing documents but also pictures, sound, and animation. Today the principal microcomputer database programs are Microsoft Access, Microsoft Visual FoxPro, and Borland's Paradox.

Communications Software

Communications software manages the transmission of data between computers. When you buy a modem, you often get communications software with it. Popular microcomputer communications programs are QuickLink and Procomm Plus. If you subscribe to an online information service such as CompuServe or America Online, the company will provide you with its own communications software.

Communications software gives you the following capabilities, among others:

- *Online connections:* You can connect to electronic bulletin board systems (BBSs) organized around special interests, to online services, and to the Internet. The software allows the microcomputer to operate in *terminal emulation mode*—that is, it allows the microcomputer to act like a terminal hooked up to a larger computer and thus gain access to it.

- *Use of financial services:* With communications software you can order discount merchandise, look up airline schedules and make reservations, follow the stock market, and even do some home banking and bill paying.

- *Remote access connections:* While traveling you can use your portable computer to exchange files via modem with your desktop computer at home.

- *File transfer:* Communications software allows users to *download* (copy to user's disk) files from remote locations and *upload* (copy to remote location's storage medium) files.

- *Fax support:* Communications software also allows users to fax messages and receive faxed messages directly from and to their microcomputers.

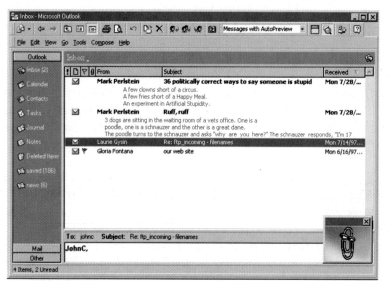

Electronic Mail Software

Electronic mail (e-mail) software enables users to send letters and documents, including graphics, from one computer to another. Many organizations have electronic mail systems, and each person is assigned a unique mailbox. If you were a sales representative, for example, such a mailbox would allow you to transmit a report you created on your word processor to a sales manager in another area. Or you could route the same message to a number of users on a distribution list. Popular e-mail software packages include Qualcomm's Eudora and Microsoft Outlook's Exchange client software.

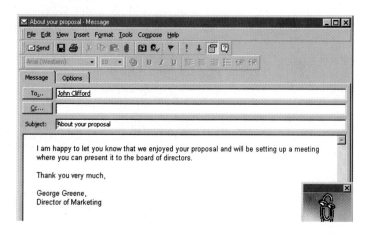

QUICK CHECK	What type of applications software would be the best suited to performing extensive calculations? managing large amounts of data?

THE INTERNET

The Internet is the world's biggest network. It can be accessed in various ways and can hook you up with virtually any resource imaginable. However, it is not necessarily easy to use without some knowledge and experience.

WHERE DID THE INTERNET COME FROM?

Called "the mother of all networks," the **Internet,** or simply "the **Net,**" is an international network connecting more than 140,000 smaller networks in more than 170 countries. These networks are formed by educational, commercial, nonprofit, government, and military entities. To connect with the Internet, you need pretty much the same things you need to connect with online information services: a computer, modem and telephone line (or other network connection), and appropriate software.

Created by the U.S. Department of Defense in 1969 (under the name ARPAnet—ARPA was the department's Advanced Research Project Agency), the Internet was built to serve two purposes. The first was to share research among military, industry, and university sources. The second was to provide a system for sustaining communication among military units in the event of nuclear attack. Thus, the system was designed to allow many routes among many computers, so that a message could arrive at its destination by many possible ways, not just a single path. This original network system was largely based on the Unix operating system.

With the many different kinds of computers being connected, engineers had to find a way for the computers to speak the same language. The solution developed was TCP/IP, the Unix communications protocol standard since 1983 and the heart of the Internet. **TCP/IP,** for **Transmission Control Protocol/Internet Protocol,** is the standardized set of computer protocols that allow different computers on different networks, using different operating systems, to communicate with each other efficiently—thus making the Internet appear to the user to operate as a single network. TCP/IP breaks data and messages into packets of information of about 1500 characters each and gives them a destination and formats them with error-protection bits. Each packet travels via the fastest route possible. On the Internet, this route may change in seconds. Thus the last packet sent may arrive first at the destination. For this reason, TCP/IP is needed to reassemble the packets into their original order. For detailed histories of the Internet, try these sites:

Hobbe's Internet Timeline—*http://info.isoc.org/guest/zakon/Internet/History/HIT.html*
History of the Internet—*http://www.Internetvalley.com/intval.html*Hobbe's Internet
NetHistory—*http://www.geocities.com/SiliconValley/2260*

As an aside: On the Internet's global computer links, communication is about 90% in English, about 5% in French, 2% in Spanish, and 3% in other languages.

CONNECTING TO THE INTERNET

There are three basic ways to connect your microcomputer with the Internet. The first is through a dedicated connection:

1. *Through school or work:* Universities, colleges, and most large businesses have dedicated, high-speed phone lines that provide a direct connection to the Internet. If you're a student, this may be the best deal, because the connection is free or low cost. However, if you live off-campus and want to get this Internet connection from home, you probably won't be able to do so. To use a direct connection, your microcomputer must have TCP/IP software and be connected to the local area network that has the direct-line connection to the Internet.

The next two types of connections are called "dial-up" connections:

2. *Through online information services:* As mentioned, subscribing to a commercial online information service, which provides you with its own communications software, may not be the cheapest way to connect to the Internet, but it may be the easiest. In this case, the online service acts as a "gateway" to the Internet. However, such services may not offer access to *all* aspects of the Internet.

3. *Through Internet service providers (ISPs):* To obtain complete access to the Internet through a dial-up connection, you use an ISP. **Internet service providers (ISPs)** are local or national companies that provide unlimited public access to the Internet and World Wide Web for a flat, monthly fee. Essentially an ISP is a small network that connects to the high-speed communications links that make up the Internet's backbone—the major supercomputer sites and educational and research foundations within the United States and throughout the world. Forrester Research Inc. predicts that ISPs could claim as many as 32 million online subscribers in the U.S. by 2000 versus 12.7 million for commercial online services. Once you have contacted an ISP and paid the required fee, the ISP will provide you with information about phone numbers for connections and about how to set up your computer and modem to dial into their network of servers. This will require dealing with some system software settings, using a user name ("userID") and a password, and typing in some other specified configuration information. Once the first connection is made, your computer will usually save the settings and other information and provide you with a shortcut method of connecting to the ISP in the future. Once you are connected to the ISP, if you are an experienced user, you can type in Unix-based commands or use

specifically designed software to navigate around the Internet. Or, if you are not an experienced Internet user, you can launch your browser software (such as Netscape) by clicking on its icon and then use the browser's graphical user interface and menus to move around the part of the Internet called the "Web" (discussed in more detail shortly).

So far, most ISPs have been small and limited in geographic coverage; the largest national company has been Netcom Online Communication Services Inc. of San Jose, Calif. Other established national ISPs are MindSpring Enterprises, Inc., UUnet Technologies, and BBN Corporation. Competitors are MCI Internet, AT&T WorldNet, and Pacific Bell Internet (all from telephone companies); and TeleCommunication Inc.'s @Home (from the cable-TV giant and pronounced "At Home"). Clearly, this is an area of fierce competition, but the presence of the phone and cable-TV companies in particular could help expand the mass market for Internet services.

You can ask someone who is already connected to the Internet to access the worldwide list of ISPs at *http://www.thelist.com.* At this site, you can view pricing data and a description of supported features for each provider in your area.

Figure 27, on the next two pages, shows a basic Internet connection. Once you're on the Net, how do you get where you want to go? That topic is next.

INTERNET ADDRESSES

To send and receive e-mail using the Internet, you need an Internet address. When Internet e-mail became fashionable, such addresses began to appear on business cards just as fax numbers did a couple of years earlier. For a while, newsmagazines such as *Time* and *Newsweek* even printed the Net addresses of writers of e-mail letters, until one complained that it exposed them to cranks (like publicizing someone's private postal mail address in a national magazine).

In the **Domain Name System (DNS),** the Internet's addressing scheme (developed in 1984), an Internet address (domain name) usually has two sections, reading left to right from the specific to the general. Consider the address

president@whitehouse.gov.us

The first section, the *userID,* tells "who" is at the address—in this case, *president,* who is the *recipient.* The second section, after the @ ("at") symbol, tells "where" the address is—*location* (which may have more than one part), *top-level domain,* and *country* (if required, such as *us* for the United States, *ca* for Canada, *cx* for Christmas Island, and *se* for Sweden); in this case, *whitehouse.gov.us.* Components of the second part of the address are separated by periods (called "dots"). *(See Figure 28 on page 50.)* Sometimes an underscore (_) is used between a recipient's first-name initials and last name, such as *s_claus@northpole.org.*

Currently there are six top-level domain types:

- *com* = commercial organizations
- *edu* = educational and research organizations
- *gov* = government organizations
- *mil* = military organizations
- *net* = gateway or host network
- *org* = nonprofit or miscellaneous organizations

Who has the authority to assign new domain names? Since 1993, Network Solutions, Inc. currently holds the National Science Foundation contract to register domain names and issue new ones. Their approximately 45 employees register about 85,000 names a month, more than 1 million names to date. Users who want their own domains pay $100 to register a name for the first two years and $50 per year after that. However, Network Solutions' contract expires in March 1998, and several groups are battling for control of the naming system. (E-mail addresses for individuals who sign up with an online service or an ISP are provided by the service; these people use the service's domain.)

NAVIGATING THE INTERNET: FEATURES AND TOOLS

The principal features of the Internet are e-mail, discussion groups, file transfer, remote access, and information searches:

- *E-mail:* The World Wide Web is getting all the headlines, but for many people the main attraction of the Internet is electronic mail. Foremost among the Internet e-mail programs is Qualcomm's Eudora software, which is also used by many educational institutions on the Internet. Eudora Light is free and comes

FIGURE 27

From your room to the world. The backbones and major arteries of the Internet are run by a group of larger network providers, often called *network providers* (*NSPs*). Users connect to local ISPs via modems, ISDN adapters, or other means (such as a school network). Local ISPs in turn connect to NSPs like, in the United States, UUNet's Alternet, IBM's Advantis, and those offered by AGIS, AT&T, MCI, and Sprint. ISPs connect to NSPs by lines leased from local telephone companies.

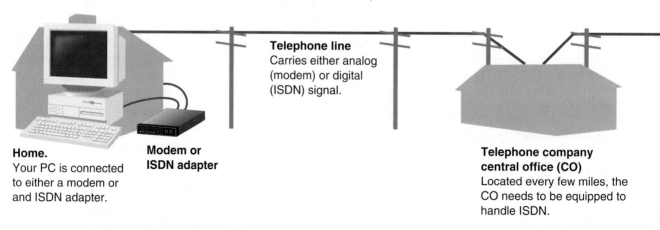

Home.
Your PC is connected to either a modem or and ISDN adapter.

Modem or ISDN adapter

Telephone line
Carries either analog (modem) or digital (ISDN) signal.

Telephone company central office (CO)
Located every few miles, the CO needs to be equipped to handle ISDN.

bundled with other Internet products. (Note that if you are using an information service such as CompuServe to connect to the Internet, you would use the service's e-mail system; thus you would not need separate e-mail software.)

- *Usenet newsgroups and electronic discussion groups:* One of the Internet's most interesting features goes under the name *usenet,* short for user network, which is essentially a giant, dispersed bulletin board. Usenet newsgroups are electronic discussion groups that focus on a specific topic, the equivalent of CompuServe's or AOL's forums. They are one of the most lively and heavily trafficked areas of the Net. Usenetters exchange e-mail and messages ("news"). Users post questions, answers, general information, and FAQ files on usenet. A **FAQ** (pronounced "fack"), for **frequently asked questions,** is a file that lays out the basics for a newsgroup's discussion. It's always best to read a newsgroup's FAQ before joining the discussion or posting (asking) questions.

There are more than 35,000 usenet newsgroup forums and they cover hundreds of topics. Examples are *rec.arts.startrek.info,soc.culture.african.american,* and *misc.jobs.offered.* The first part, in these examples, is the recipient group: *rec* for recreation, *soc* for social issues, *comp* for computers, *biz* for business, *sci* for science, *misc* for miscellaneous. The next part is the subject: for example, *rec.food.cooking.* The category called *alt* newsgroups offers more free-form topics (one might say "alternative" lifestyles), such as *alt.rock-n-roll.metal* or *alt.internet.services.*

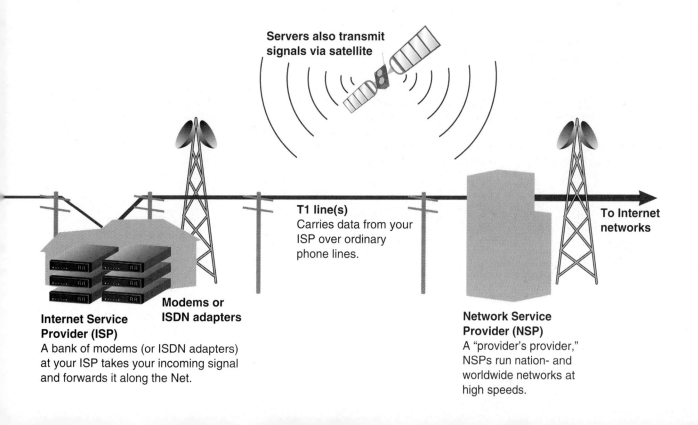

Servers also transmit signals via satellite

T1 line(s)
Carries data from your ISP over ordinary phone lines.

To Internet networks

Modems or ISDN adapters

Internet Service Provider (ISP)
A bank of modems (or ISDN adapters) at your ISP takes your incoming signal and forwards it along the Net.

Network Service Provider (NSP)
A "provider's provider," NSPs run nation- and worldwide networks at high speeds.

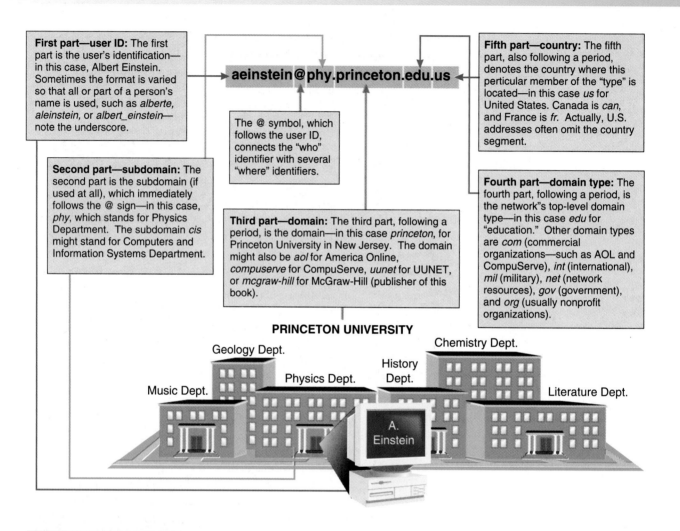

First part—user ID: The first part is the user's identification—in this case, Albert Einstein. Sometimes the format is varied so that all or part of a person's name is used, such as *alberte, aleinstein,* or *albert_einstein*—note the underscore.

Second part—subdomain: The second part is the subdomain (if used at all), which immediately follows the @ sign—in this case, *phy*, which stands for Physics Department. The subdomain *cis* might stand for Computers and Information Systems Department.

The @ symbol, which follows the user ID, connects the "who" identifier with several "where" identifiers.

Third part—domain: The third part, following a period, is the domain—in this case *princeton*, for Princeton University in New Jersey. The domain might also be *aol* for America Online, *compuserve* for CompuServe, *uunet* for UUNET, or *mcgraw-hill* for McGraw-Hill (publisher of this book).

Fifth part—country: The fifth part, also following a period, denotes the country where this particular member of the "type" is located—in this case *us* for United States. Canada is *can*, and France is *fr*. Actually, U.S. addresses often omit the country segment.

Fourth part—domain type: The fourth part, following a period, is the network's top-level domain type—in this case *edu* for "education." Other domain types are *com* (commercial organizations—such as AOL and CompuServe), *int* (international), *mil* (military), *net* (network resources), *gov* (government), and *org* (usually nonprofit organizations).

aeinstein@phy.princeton.edu.us

PRINCETON UNIVERSITY

Geology Dept.   Chemistry Dept.
Physics Dept.   History Dept.
Music Dept.   Literature Dept.
A. Einstein

FIGURE 28

What an Internet address means. How an e-mail message might find its way across the Internet to a hypothetical address for Albert Einstein in the Physics Department of Princeton University.

- *Mailing lists and e-mail-based discussion groups:* Combining e-mail news-groups, mailing lists—called *listservs*—allow you to subscribe (generally free) to an e-mail mailing list on a particular subject or subjects. The mailing-list sponsor then sends the identical message to everyone on that list. Thus the newsgroup listserv messages automatically appear in your mailbox—you do not have to access the newsgroup. There are more than 3000-plus electronic mailing-list discussion groups. (Subscribers to mailing lists need to check and download/delete mail almost every day; otherwise their mailboxes will become "full.")

- *FTP—for copying all the free files you want:* Many Net users enjoy "FTPing," cruising the system and checking into some of the tens of thousands of so-called FTP sites offering interesting free files and programs to copy (download). **FTP, for File Transfer Protocol,** is a method whereby you can connect to a remote computer called an *FTP site* and transfer publicly available files to your microcomputer's hard disk. The free files offered cover nearly anything that can be stored on a computer: software, games, photos, maps, art, music, books, statistics. Some 2000-plus FTP sites (so-called *anonymous FTP sites*) are open to anyone; others can be accessed only by knowing a password. You can also use FTP to upload your files to an FTP site. (Not all FTP sites are free to download; for example, the software patches, or upgrades, we mentioned earlier are not free.)

  If you know an FTP file's name or partial name, you can use an Internet software utility called *ARCHIE* (ARCHIvE) to help find the file. There are more than 30 computer systems throughout the Internet that maintain Archie servers, which keep catalogs of files for downloading from FTP sites. The Archie servers periodically update their lists. Once you find a file's location, you can use the FTP feature to download it using your e-mail address and a sign-in name. Many other FTP programs exist. Many ISPs and information services, as well as Web browsers, offer FTP programs to their users.

- *Telnet—to connect to remote computers:* **Telnet** is a terminal emulation protocol that allows you to use an Internet account to connect (log on) to remote computers as if you were directly connected to those computers instead of, for example, through your ISP site. Once you are logged on, everything you see on the screen and everything you can do is controlled by programs running on the host system. This feature, which allows microcomputers to communicate successfully with mainframes, is especially useful for perusing large databases and library card catalogs. There are perhaps 1000 Telnet-accessible library catalogs, and a few thousand more Internet sites around the world have Telnet interfaces. (Telnet is a text-only means of communication.) Telnet programs are also usually provided by ISPs and information services, as well as some operating systems.

- *Gopherspace, including Veronica and Jughead—the easy menu system:* Several software tools exist to help sift through the staggering amount of information on the Internet, but one of the most important is *Gopher.* Gopher, one of the older Internet protocols along with Telnet and FTP, is a uniform system of menus, or series of lists, that allows users to easily search for and retrieve files stored on different computers. Why is it called "Gopher"? Because the first gopher was developed at the home of the Golden Gophers, the University of Minnesota, and it helps you "go fer" the files you seek. There are thousands of gopher servers hooked up to the Internet "Gopherspace."

A classic running joke on the Internet is the use of puns on cartoon character names, such as those in the "Archie" comics. It started with Archie, and then the developers of a search application for Gopherspace concocted *Veronica* (for *Very Easy Rodent-Oriented Net-wide Index to Computerized Archives*). Veronica is a tool to help you search a large collection of Gopher menus for the keyword you specify. Jughead does the same thing only it searches just the Gopher menu at the particular site you are currently visiting. (Jughead was developed at the University of Utah by Rhett "Jonzy" Jones and stands for Jonzy's Universal Gopher Hierarchy Excavation And Display.)

- *WAIS—ways of searching by content:* Pronounced "ways" ("wayz"), *WAIS,* for *Wide Area Information Server,* is a database on the Internet that contains indexes of documents that reside on the Internet. It facilitates searching other Internet databases by contents, using specific words or phrases rather than sorting through a hierarchy of menus. Unfortunately, WAIS is offered only by certain information sites (servers) and so can be applied to only a limited number of files.

Figure 29 shows some of what's available on the Internet.

One last feature of the Internet remains to be discussed—for most users, perhaps the most important one: the World Wide Web

---

QUICK CHECK   **What are the main purposes you think you will use the Internet for?**

WORLD WIDE WEB

The Internet itself is not designed for sound and video. So why are we reading about multimedia on the Internet? The answer lies with the fastest-growing part of the Internet—many times larger than any online service—the World Wide Web. This is the most graphically inviting and easily navigable section of the Internet. The **World Wide Web,** or simply the **Web,** consists of an interconnected (hyperlinked) system of sites, servers all over the world that can store information in multimedia form—sounds, photos, video, as well as text. The system is called the Web because the screens you see in rapid sequence from various files may be on different computers all over the world.

Note three distinctive features:

1. The Web subsumes Internet information systems such as Gopher and FTP. These resources can still be accessed through the Web, but the Web provides a wealth of additional capabilities not previously offered by these more restricted connection methods.

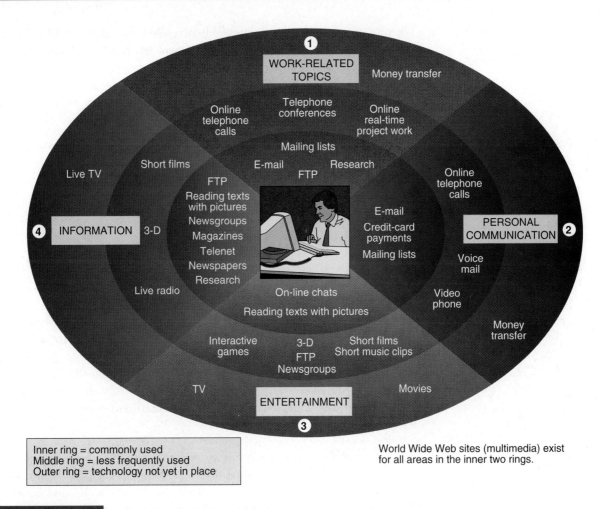

Inner ring = commonly used
Middle ring = less frequently used
Outer ring = technology not yet in place

World Wide Web sites (multimedia) exist
for all areas in the inner two rings.

FIGURE 29   What's available on the Internet

2. Whereas Archie, Gopher, and WAIS deal with text, the Web provides information in *multimedia* form—graphics, video, and audio as well as text.

3. Whereas Gopher is a menu-based approach to accessing Net resources, the Web uses a hypertext format. *Hypertext* is a system in which documents scattered across many Internet sites are directly linked, so that a word or phrase in one document becomes a connection to a document in a different place. The format, or language, used for files on the Web is called **hypertext mark-up language (HTML).** The protocol for transferring HTML files is **hypertext transfer protocol (HTTP).** (Web software was developed in 1990 by Tim Berners-Lee at CERN, in Geneva, Switzerland. CERN stands for Centre European pour la Recherche Nucleaire.) When you use your mouse to point-and-click on a hypertext link (a highlighted or underlined word or phrase), it may become a doorway to another place within the same document or to another document on a computer thousands of miles away.

The places you might visit on the Web are called *Web sites,* and the estimated number of such sites throughout the world ranges up to 1,250,000. More specifically, a **Web site** is a file or files stored on a computer (Web server). For example, the Parents Place Web site address *(http://www.parents.com)* is a resource run by mothers and fathers that includes links to other related sites, such as the Computer Museum Guide to the Best Software for Kids and the National Parenting Center.

Information on a Web site is stored on "pages." The **home page** is the main page of first screen you see when you access a Web site, but there are often other pages or screens. "Web site" and "home page" tend to be used interchangeably, although a site may have many pages. (Some of them are simply abandoned because their creators have not updated or deleted them, the online equivalent of space-age debris orbiting the earth.)

To access a Web site (home page), you use Web browser software and the site's address, called a *URL (Universal Resource Locater).* A **Web browser** is a graphical-user interface software that translates HTML documents and allows you to view Web pages on your computer screen. The main Web browsers are Netscape Navigator and Microsoft Internet Explorer. Others include HotJava and Mosaic. With the browser, you can browse (search through) the Web. When you connect with a particular Web site, the screen full of information (the home page) is sent to you. You can easily skip from one page to another by using your mouse to click on the hyperlinks, indicated by text that is underlined or highlighted, or by graphics.

To locate a Web site, you type in its address, or **URL,** for **Uniform Resource Locator.** Often it looks something like this: *http://www.blah.blah.html* (*http* stands for "hypertext transfer protocol," *www* for "World Wide Web," and *html* for "hypertext mark-up language.") In many cases you can omit the *http://* and just start with *www.* (*Note:* In URLs, as well as in domain-type Internet addresses, lowercase and capital letters should be typed in as such—this relates to the underlying Unix structure of the Internet. Also, URLs *do* change; if you get a "cannot locate server" message, try using a search engine to locate the site at its new address.) Figure 30 illustrates the various components of Web pages and URLs.

Note that anyone can have a home page. Professional Web page designers can do it for you, or you can do it yourself using a menu-driven program included with your Web browser software (such as with Netscape) or using a stand-alone Web-page design software package such as Microsoft FrontPage. Once your home page is designed, complete with links, you can either let it reside on your hard disk—in which case you will have to leave your computer and your modem turned on all the time, tying up your equipment and allowing only one user access at a time—or you can rent space on your ISP's server. In the latter case, after you have designed your page(s), your ISP will give you directions about how to modem your page file to their server. (The ISP will charge you according to how many megabytes of space your file takes up on their server.)

FIGURE 30

Common examples of Web page components and hyperlinks (underlined items that will take you to new Web pages).

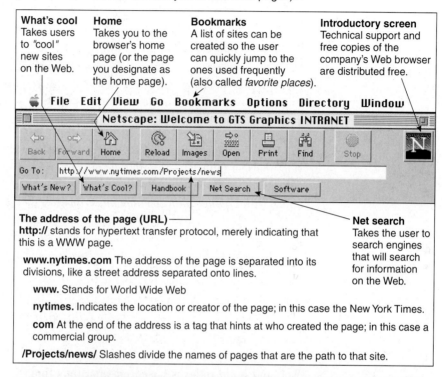

What's cool
Takes users to "cool" new sites on the Web.

Home
Takes you to the browser's home page (or the page you designate as the home page).

Bookmarks
A list of sites can be created so the user can quickly jump to the ones used frequently (also called *favorite places*).

Introductory screen
Technical support and free copies of the company's Web browser are distributed free.

The address of the page (URL)
http:// stands for hypertext transfer protocol, merely indicating that this is a WWW page.

www.nytimes.com The address of the page is separated into its divisions, like a street address separated onto lines.

> **www.** Stands for World Wide Web

> **nytimes.** Indicates the location or creator of the page; in this case the New York Times.

> **com** At the end of the address is a tag that hints at who created the page; in this case a commercial group.

/Projects/news/ Slashes divide the names of pages that are the path to that site.

Net search
Takes the user to search engines that will search for information on the Web.

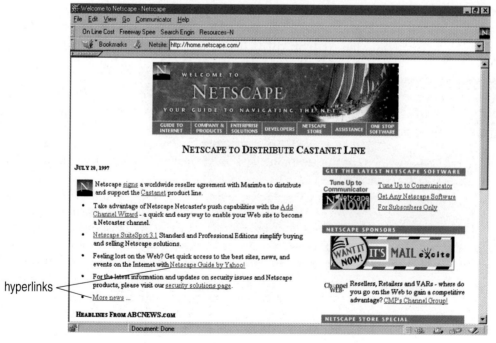

hyperlinks

WHAT CAN YOU FIND ON THE WEB?

It's hard to conceive of how much information is available on the Web. Of course, you can obtain many of the services offered by online information services by accessing the URLs of, for example, travel agents, financial investment groups, restaurant guides, mail-order shopping sites, free software download sites, and so on. You can also read online versions of newspapers and magazines (called *e-zines*). (*Note:* Heavy-duty database research will still require some Archie-type and FTP Internet navigation or the use of an information service's connection to research databases.) But there are many more places to go.

But how do you find these places? First, several books are available, updated every year, that list the URLs of hundreds of popular Web sites, for example, *1001 Really Cool Web Sites* from Jamsa Press. Sites listed include Best of the Web Award Recipients *(http://wings.buffalo.edu/contest/awards/)*, Library of Congress Cultural Exhibits *(http://lcweb.loc.gov/homepage/exhibits.html)*, The Nine Planets: A Multimedia Tour of the Solar system *(http://seds.lpl.arizona.edu/billa/tnp)*, Stock Market Data from MIT *(http://www.ai.mit.edu/stocks)*, and Physicians for Social Responsibility *(http://www.pst.org:8000)*.

Second you can use a Web search engine or directory to locate the URLs of sites on topics that interest you. *Search engines* find Web pages on their own; *directories* are created by people submitting Web sites to a group that classifies and indexes them. Search engines use software *spiders* (indexers) to "crawl" around the Web and build indexes based on what they find.

Web browsers allow you to quickly use search engines and directories by clicking the NET SEARCH button and then clicking on the icon of the engine/directory you want to use. Web browsers also allow you to type in the directories' URLs, for example, under the "Open location" option on the "File" menu.

Some popular engines and directories are the following:

●*Alta Vista:* The most popular search engine on the Web is Digital's Alta Vista site: *www.altavista.digital.com.*

- *Excite NetSearch (http://www.excite.com/):* Excite differs from other Web index services in that it returns not only a list of sites and articles in which the keywords you specified appear but also a list of relevant pages based on "concept" by analyzing words in a document. In addition, it ranks the documents as to how well they fit your original search criteria.

- *InfoSeek (http://www.infoseek.com/)* ranks results according to relevance to your search criteria. InfoSeek also searches more than the Web, indexing Usenet newsnet newsgroups and several non-Internet databases.

- *Lycos (http://www.lycos.com/)* offers a list of interesting Web sites called A2Z, which indicates the most popular pages on the Web, as measured by the number of hypertext links, or "hits," from other Web sites pointing to them.

- *Yahoo! (http://www.yahoo.com/)* is one of the most popular Web directories and lists not only Web pages but also Usenet newsgroups, Gophers, and FTP sites. Among other things, it features a weekly list of "cool sites" and headline news from the wire service Reuters.

- *Argus/University of Michigan Subject-Oriented Clearinghouse (http://www.lib.umich.edu/chhome.html)* is a directory of directories. It provides a list of subject-specific directories on topics ranging from arts and entertainment to social science and social issues. For example, if you're interested in art, you would see it lists *World Wide Arts Resources (http://www.concourse.com/wwar/default.html),* which has links to many museums and galleries and an index of more than 2000 artists. (Besides material on the Web, Argus also lists information in FTP servers and Gopher sites.)

You can also purchase Web search utilities, software tools that you can install on your microcomputer that orchestrate simultaneous, intelligent queries in multiple Web search engines. Examples are Quarterdeck WebCompass, ForeFront Group WebSeeker, Symantec Internet FastFind, Tympani NetAttaché, and Iconovex EchoSearch.

THINKING AHEAD

"We should all be concerned about the future," said engineer and inventor Charles Kettering, "because we will have to spend the rest of our lives there." *Convergence* is definitely part of our future. Basically, **digital convergence** is the technological merger of several industries through various devices that exchange information in the digital format used by computers. The industries are computers, communications, consumer electronics, entertainment, and mass media.

Technological convergence has tremendous significance. It means that, from a common electronic base, information can be communicated in all the ways we are accustomed to receiving it. These include the familiar media of newspapers, photographs, films, recordings, radio, and television. However, it can also be communicated through newer technology—satellite, cable, cellular phone, fax machine, or compact disk, for example. More important, as time goes on, *the same information may be exchanged among many kinds of equipment, using the language of computers.* Understanding this shift from single, isolated technologies to a unified digital technology means understanding the effects of this convergence on your life.

KEY TERMS

EXERCISES

SHORT ANSWER

1. Briefly describe the function of each of the six main components of a computer system.

2. What is the function of the system unit in a computer system?

3. What is the difference between system software and applications software?

4. How is the amount of main memory in a computer related to its performance?

5. Briefly describe the types of activities you can perform on the Internet.

6. What is a motherboard?

7. Why does a computer require system software?

8. What is the significance of the terms *track* and *sector*?

9. What is a coprocessor chip? What is the purpose of a graphics coprocessor chip?

10. Why don't programmers write programs in machine language?

TRUE/FALSE

1. Main memory is a software component. (true or false)

2. System software tells the computer how to handle the keyboard and other hardware components. (true or false)

3. A local area network connects computers in an office or a building. (true or false)

4. The biggest network in the world is the Internet. (true or false)

5. A safe and convenient place for storing floppy diskettes is in a holder that is attached to your monitor. (true or false)

6. A modem is necessary to allow a computer to send data across telephone lines. (true or false)

7. Applications software starts up the computer and functions as the principal coordinator of all hardware components. (true or false)

8. The *.com* domain is the default type and it stands for "common." (true or false)

9. To access data stored on a diskette, you can use a scanner if a diskette drive is not available. (true or false)

10. On a computer screen, the more pixels that appear per square inch, the higher the resolution and clearer the image. (true or false)

MULTIPLE CHOICE

1. Which of the following is not considered a peripheral hardware device?

   a. keyboard

   b. scanner

   c. monitor

   d. printer

   e. memory

2. Which of the following can translate drawings and photos into digital form?

   a. keyboard

   b. mouse

   c. scanner

   d. modem

   e. trackball

3. Which of the following enables digital data to be transmitted over the phone lines?

   a. keyboard

   b. mouse

   c. scanner

   d. modem

   e. trackball

4. Which hardware category does a scanner fall into?

   a. input

   b. processing and memory

   c. output

   d. storage

   e. communications

5. _____ software is loaded upon booting and controls the computer's resources.

   a. Applications

   b. System

   c. Word processing

   d. Spreadsheet

   e. Database

6. The category of hardware that can be compared to a filing cabinet is _____ hardware.

   a. input

   b. processing

   c. storage

   d. output

   e. communications

7. Which of the following is used to temporarily hold text when it is copied from one application to another?

   a. Clipboard

   b. word processing software

   c. graphics software

   d. spreadsheet software

   e. database software

8. All diskettes must be _____ before they can store data.

   a. processed

   b. input

   c. output

   d. formatted

   e. initiated

9. Which of the following isn't related to the screen clarity of a CRT?

   a. resolution

   b. dot pitch

   c. refresh rate

   d. liquid crystal

   e. coprocessor

KNOWLEDGE IN ACTION

1. Determine what types of computers are being used where you work or go to school. Microcomputers? Workstations? Minicomputers? Any mainframe or supercomputers? In which departments are the different types of computers used? What are they being used for? How are they connected to other computers?

2. What system software is used on the computer at your school, work, or home? Why was this software selected? Do you find this software easy to use?

3. Picture yourself in your future job. What types of current applications software do you see yourself using? What are you producing with this software? What kinds of new applications software would you invent to help you do your job better?

4. What types of storage hardware are currently being used in the computer you use at school or at work? What is the storage capacity of these hardware devices? Would you recommend alternate storage hardware be used? Why or why not?

5. If you could buy any printer you want, what type (make, model, etc.) would you choose? Does the printer need to fit into a small space? Does it need to print across the width of wide paper 11 × 14 inches)? In color? On multi-carbon forms? Review some of the current computer publications for articles or advertisements relating to printers. How much does the printer cost? Your needs should be able to justify the cost of the printer (if necessary, make up what your needs might be).

6. Describe the latest microprocessor chip released by Intel. Who are the intended users of this chip? How is this chip better than its predecessor? Perform your research using current computer magazines and periodicals and/or the Internet.

7. Look through some computer magazines and identify advertised microcomputer systems. Decide which microcomputer might be the best one for you based on your processing requirements (if necessary, pick a hypothetical project and identify some probable processing requirements). Describe the microcomputer you would choose and why. Compare this microcomputer to others you saw advertised using the following categories: (a) name and brand of computer, (b) microprocessor, (c) RAM capacity, (d) availability of cache memory, and (e) cost.

BROOKE CALL ME WHEN YOU GET TO # 6

Index